My Life In Football

YOU MUST
BE JOACHIM

Julian Joachim

First Edition.
First published 2021

Published by:
Morgan Lawrence Publishing Services Limited
16a Main Ridge
West Boston
PE21 6QQ
www.morganlawrence.co.uk
email: info@morganlawrence.co.uk
Company number: 12910264

(C) Julian Joachim & Mathew Mann, 2021

ISBN: 978183823931

A CIP catalogue record is available from the British Library.

Photographs are courtesy of:
PA Images/Alamy Stock Photo, Allstar Picture Library Ltd,
REUTERS, BPM Media, Jim Brown, Coventry City FC, Andrew
Varley, Leeds United FC, Ray Simpson, Darlington FC, Paul
Joannou, Walsall FC.

Cover design by LCGraphix. Cover photograph by Andrew Varley.
Typesetting by Mathew Mann
Proofreading by Lois Hide

Printed and bound in Bulgaria by Pulsio Print.

Contents

Roofing & Builders

Presented by
Clive Turner

T: 0116 2419137   M: 07860 419137
E: roofingandbuilders@hotmail.com
Safe Construction (LEICESTER) LTD
10 Pulford Drive, Scraptoft, Leicester LE7 9UD

What we do

Re-Roofs / New Roofs / Flat Roofs / Factory Cladding
Roofs / Flat Roof to Pitch Roof Conversion /
Roof Repairs / Slating & Tiling / Extensions /
Ventilation Systems / Conservatories / Porches /
Garden Walls / Chimneys Reduced or Rebuilt or
Repointed   / Block Paving / Windows /
Fitted Kitchens / New UPVC Gutters & Facias Etc.

Sponsors introduction

Introduction by Clive Turner. Director of Safe Construction (LEICESTER) Limited.

In the early seventies, the highlight of my week was standing in the Main Stand at Filbert Street watching Frank Worthington, Alan Birchenall, Keith Weller and the rest of the Bloomfield Boys taking on English football's elite. Although that particular Leicester City team didn't win any trophies, they were one of the most entertaining sides in the country. I thought they were incredible.

Frank Worthington was my idol; a player blessed with natural ability on the pitch and a flamboyant character off it. When I was 11, Frank lived on Scraptoft Lane, round the corner from my house, and I remember going out carol singing one Christmas evening and knocking on his front door. His Mrs answered and then Frankie walked over and stood behind her. I belted out We Three Kings and he made me sing it all the way through before handing me a shiny 50p piece – a fortune to an 11-year-old at the time.

Fast forward twenty years and I found a new Filbert Street hero. Like many other Leicester City fans, I remember Julian bursting onto the scene in the 1992/93 season, as one of the most exciting players ever to play for the Foxes.

I was at Oakwell in 1993 to witness Julian's wonder goal in the FA Cup and, later that season, I was in the stands at the City Ground when he ran half the length of the pitch to score another wondergoal against Portsmouth in the play off semi final.

The following year, I met Julian for the first time at Rex William's Snooker Club on Narborough Road, Leicester. I was there with my brother, Phil, when Julian and Scott Eustace, another young Leicester City player, walked in. Phil and his mates wrote the Leicester City fanzine *Where's The Money Gone?* and knew Julian well, so I was introduced to him, and we played a few frames of snooker.

I have so many memories of him tearing defences to shreds during those fantastic 'Wembley Years' of the nineties and I was gutted to see him leave Leicester to join Aston Villa. I kept a close eye on his career and enjoyed watching him develop into a top Premier League player.

I met Julian again in 2008, when he was approaching the end of his professional career, because Dylan, my friend Tony's son, began dating Jazzy, Julian's daughter. We became firm friends and Julian helps me out now and again with my roofing and building business, Safe Construction (LEICESTER) Limited, and that's when I really got to know him.

Julian is a lovely lad with a fascinating story to tell and I am pleased that he has finally decided to write his autobiography. I know that this book will be a very interesting read for fans of all his former clubs, and football fans in general, and I am delighted to sponsor Julian's autobiography and wish him every success.

Enjoy the book.

Foreword
By Mark Draper

I first met Julian – or Jockey as he was known – when I signed for Leicester City in 1994. Although he was only 19, Jockey already had a big reputation; he had been capped at England under 21 level and he boasted a highlight reel of unbelievable goals. I was looking forward to playing with him and his presence in the squad was a major factor in my decision to sign for City.

Jockey's immense talent was evident in training and during pre-season, but I remember the first time I saw what he was really capable of. It was September 1994 and we were searching for our first Premier League win when big-spending Tottenham came to Filbert Street. No one gave us a chance against our high-profile opponents who lined up with Sol Campbell, Jurgen Klinsmann and Darren Anderton, but we beat them convincingly, 3-1. Julian set up one and scored the other two and he could have scored four – he was that good. It was scary watching what he could do against top Premier League defenders.

Sadly, Leicester were relegated at the end of that season and I moved to Aston Villa as I wanted to stay in the Premier League. I kept in touch with Jockey and in March 1996, he phoned me to say that he'd been offered a move to Villa Park and wanted my advice. I told him to come, 100%. We had a fantastic side with a great manager in Brian Little, and I knew he'd do well for us, and he did.

Off the pitch, he is a very quiet, shy person who keeps himself to himself. While some of the lads were quite rowdy, Julian was happy sitting in the dressing room lost in his own thoughts, chuckling away.

I haven't got a bad word to say about him. Well, actually that's not true!

We used to travel into training and matches together and always had a good laugh, but he was always liable to drop a fart in the car and they were awful!

If I had to describe him in two words, I'd use silent assassin – especially at cards! I was in the card school at Villa along with Julian, Tommy Johnson, Dwight Yorke and Mark Bosnich. We used to play everywhere and anywhere, for as long as we could. Jockey was the more experienced card player and always had a knowing little smile on his face as he placed his bets.

It's no secret that Jockey liked a flutter on the horses, and he made me laugh when he compared himself to a racehorse, saying that he preferred playing when the ground was firm or good to firm, rather than soft! Once he got moving there was no one quicker than him and even the best defenders in the world struggled with his pace and power. He was the most frightening player I have seen over ten yards.

During his first few seasons at Villa, Julian was in and out of the team, but when Yorkey left to go to Manchester United in 1998, Jockey stepped up and enjoyed the best season of his career, finishing as our top goal scorer and winning the Player of the Year award. There are so many games where I'd watch him breeze past two or three players and I'd just think, wow.

Julian had a fantastic career at the top level and I firmly believe that if he'd been a little more consistent he'd have played for England.

As a footballer. you cross paths with many people and it is rare to keep in touch with your former teammates, but Jockey and I have remained friends for almost thirty years. We don't see each other as much as we'd like, but we chat regularly on the phone.

Jockey is a genuine, down to earth lad and I'm honoured that he's asked me to write the foreword to his autobiography.

I hope you enjoy the book.

Mark Draper
Former Leicester City and Aston Villa midfielder.

CHAPTER 1
Chasing chickens and kung fu fighting

On 20th September 1974, Carl Douglas was top of the UK charts singing "Everyone was Kung Fu Fighting." Meanwhile, my mum was having a fight of a different kind in Peterborough Maternity Hospital. After a long labour, I finally entered the world weighing in at seven pounds eight ounces. I was named Julian Kevin Joachim. My mum, Janie James, had worked in a factory since she left school and later become a full-time carer to my nan. My dad, Ennis Joachim, was born in the beautiful Caribbean island of Saint Vincent and the Grenadines and moved to England in 1967 when he was nineteen. His first job in the UK was as a steel worker and he eventually took employment at the McCain food factory in Whittlesey, Peterborough.

I was mum's first child, but dad already had a son, Mark, a few months older than me. If you do the maths, it's not surprising that my parents separated when I was just weeks old, so Mum and I went to live with my nan in Boston and that is where I was brought up. Though I was born in Peterborough, I regard myself as a Bostonian.

Dad remained in Peterborough and moved in with his ex (Mark's mum) and they went on to have two more children, Charlene and Ashley. It was difficult growing up without a father in my daily life. During the school holidays I went back to Peterborough and stayed with my nan, dad's mum. Dad would pop over to see me and sometimes Charlene would be there too, but not often, so I wasn't particularly close to any of my siblings. It's not that we clashed or anything like that, we just didn't really ever get to know each other. Tragically, Ashley died while he was still in secondary school which was really sad for all of us. I speak to Mark and Charlene now and again these days which is nice and I have a similar relationship with dad. We might not speak for two or three years and then we'll touch base and pick up exactly where we left off. That's just how we are. He's back in Saint Vincent and the Grenadines now and, ironically, we are closer these days than ever before.

I lived at 18 Taverner Road on a council estate in Boston and as a single parent family we didn't have a lot and it was tough. Life was a struggle in all honesty, but there was a lot of love in our house. Mum was one of thirteen children and her brothers and sisters had loads of kids, so I was always surrounded by family; cousins, uncles and aunts.

When I turned five, I attended Carlton Road Primary School and enjoyed the routine of classes and learning new things. Workwise, it was pretty easy, but I struggled with discipline. I have a very laid-back attitude these days, but when I was a kid, I was a right little so and so. I guess because I grew up as an only child, I was used to getting my own way and I could be a bit of a handful at times. I didn't really understand the challenges that mum faced and I was a bit selfish to be honest. If I didn't get my own way, I'd kick off because I had a short fuse. I was a very naughty kid and always in trouble. The estate I lived on was rough and me and my mates were always getting up to mischief. Sometimes it wasn't our fault, but if I'm honest, we often went out looking for trouble. Out of boredom, we formed a gang and had scraps with other gangs. Coming from a council estate, we always felt we had a point to prove and I learnt that I had to fight and battle for everything that I wanted.

And there was nothing I wanted more than becoming a professional footballer. I know it's a cliche, but I don't remember a time when I didn't have a ball at my feet.

Like most kids growing up in the eighties, I supported the all-conquering Liverpool team, featuring the great Kenny Dalglish and Ian Rush. Watford was my second team and the reason for that was John Barnes. What a player he was; he had everything, pace, skill and was a good finisher. That goal he scored for England against Brazil in the Maracanã was unbelievable. When he signed for Liverpool, it was perfect for me.

I always did the homework that my teachers set me, but football was my priority. I played for my primary school team, although unlike my friends, I wasn't allowed to join a Sunday side as we didn't have a car and there weren't any clubs within walking distance of my home. I was disappointed but that was that, I just had to wait until I was older.

Once I got to Kitwood Boys Secondary School, I signed for Wyberton Colts as mum allowed me to walk the ten-mile round trip to the ground and back. It was a long way for my 11-year-old legs, but I didn't mind the travel as Wyberton were one of the top teams in the area with a history of producing professional footballers, including Chris Wood, the England goalkeeper at the time, so I knew they were the right club for me to try and achieve my dream.

I was always confident in my ability and I knew, even at that age, that I was good and better than most. I was quick, direct and loved nothing more than taking people on. When playing for the Colts, there were some games where I got the ball at kick off and just took on the entire team before scoring. I loved it.

David Hallam and Tim Lennon were the joint managers, and they were great, giving me encouragement and advice. I was so good that I had to play with the older teams because opposing managers complained when I played with my own age group!

It wasn't long before I was scouted and I attended my first trial when I was 12 at nearby Norwich City. I didn't get in and I was gutted. One of my Colts' teammates also had a trial and I later heard that his dad had told Norwich that I wasn't reliable enough and that I had an attitude problem. That wasn't true, but his son was also a centre forward, so with me out of the picture, it opened up the door for him. I don't blame the dad at all though, he was just trying to look after his lad.

By the time I had turned 13, I was selected for Wyberton's senior team in the men's league. They were a good team and played in a competitive division. One of my teammates was Ian Nimmo, a Boston born striker who'd played league football for Sheffield Wednesday and Doncaster during the early eighties. While at Doncaster, Nimmo was a teammate of Alan Little, whose brother, Brian, was a huge influence on my career.

I remember my senior debut like it was yesterday. My name had been mentioned in the local paper a few times, so our opponents had heard all about me and there was a decent crowd to see how this small, young kid would fare against fully grown men. The only boots that I owned were studs which were not ideal on the rock hard pitch, but in those days not many kids were fortunate enough to own both moulded and studs. To be honest, I was just grateful to have a pair of boots.

We kicked off and the ball was passed back to me. I went to control the ball, slipped and stumbled. The opponents began to laugh at me, but I managed to stand up again, got the ball back under control and weaved some of my magic. I took it past one player, then another and another before slotting the ball into the back of the net. No one laughed at me after that.

I had no fear in those days and I didn't respect anyone. I was young and thought that I'd been there and done it all already. I was playing with and against grown men but that didn't bother me one bit. I just saw it as a bigger challenge. And the bigger the challenge, the better I played.

By the time I celebrated my 14th birthday I knew that I would be a footballer, nothing was going to stop me. My heart was set on playing professionally and school had moved a long way down my list of priorities. I could have done a hell of a lot better at school, but I just didn't see the point. How was maths going to help me to become a footballer?

I went to an all-boys' school and we always had a laugh and a giggle as you can imagine and I messed about a lot. There were even a few classes that I wasn't allowed to attend because of my poor behaviour. Instead, I had to go to the Head of Year's office to do my work so that he could keep a close eye on me. My art teacher once banned me from his class for messing around, telling me, "Your brains are in your feet, lad." I took it as a compliment!

Mum and nan weren't impressed with my school reports, but they were incredibly supportive and encouraged me in my pursuit of a career in football. If I needed some new boots, they would scrimp and save to get me some, although they wouldn't really be new boots, they'd be second hand ones that we picked up from a car boot or a jumble sale. If I desperately needed something and mum couldn't afford it, she'd call dad and he'd send some money. It didn't happen very often though as mum just tried to get on with it.

When money was really tight for us, I would take a week or two off school to go out and earn a few quid. I worked the land for my uncle Charlie, sadly no longer with us, who was a gangmaster. I did everything; brussels sprout pulling, flower picking, all kinds of farm work. I even did chicken catching a few times. There were thousands and I had to chase them around, pick them up by their feet and load them onto the lorries so that they could be taken to the factories. You have to be fast to catch chickens and that might be where I got my pace from!

Chicken catching aside, I didn't really do any football training or have proper coaching sessions back then. Me and my friends were probably uncoachable anyway, as we felt that we already knew everything. Looking back now, I didn't have a clue about the game or tactics, I just played for fun. I was quick and skilful and most of what I did was off the cuff, playing on instinct really, so I didn't have to think about what I was doing.

My 'training' was playing out on the streets of Boston with my mates wherever we could find some grass. In the pre-computer game days, everyone would come out and play, often 20 or 30 a side. Those matches helped my development as with that many people you didn't get the ball often, so when you did, you learnt to keep it. Maybe proper training would have helped me, but I found it boring to kick a ball against a wall and work on my weaker foot. To be honest, if I'd tried it, I'd have been sent on my way and told to find some grass anyway!

What I enjoyed most was playing games and I was getting plenty; Saturdays with Wyberton men's team and Sundays with the under 16s. I had so much confidence in my ability and I knew that I had something in me that was different to the other lads. Boston was a small town and my name was being mentioned a lot by the local media which was really encouraging. Wyberton always had scouts sniffing around and when I was 14 I was invited to a trial at Grimsby Town who were the closest league club to me. I trained with them for a bit on an informal basis which meant that I was able to continue playing for Wyberton Colts.

After one match for the Colts, as I was coming off the pitch a guy approached me and introduced himself as Les Grey, a scout from Leicester City. He passed me his card, took my details and then came to my house to meet with mum and nan. He invited

13

me to a trial and when he found out that we didn't have a car, he offered to pick me up and take me to Belvoir Drive, City's training ground. I hadn't signed anything for Grimsby and they hadn't offered me schoolboy forms, so I was free to speak to other teams. Leicester were a massive club with a reputation for giving young players a chance and I was very interested.

At the trial my first observation was that the players were much better than those I was used to playing against. The standard was higher, but I remained confident in my ability and just played my normal game. I did well enough to be invited back for a second, and then a third trial. After my third visit, I knew that Leicester were the club for me. Everything about the place, from the facilities to the coaches, just felt right. Neville Hamilton, the Head Coach of the School of Excellence, as it was known then, offered me schoolboy forms and I signed immediately. I then received offers from Derby County and Nottingham Forest, both top- flight clubs, but I turned them down because I was, even in those days, a man of my word.

The coaching at Leicester City was exceptional. Sammy Chapman was a City scout who also coached the young lads and he played a huge part in my development. I remember he used to instruct my teammates, "Every time you get the ball, pass it to Joachim." He'd then tell me, in his broad Irish accent, "You dribble with the ball and run at the defence. Don't pass it or I'll take you off!" He gave me the confidence to play my usual game and I followed his advice for the rest of my career.

My next aim was to earn a youth contract with City by the time I finished school. I never doubted that I had the ability to make it on the pitch, but I got arrested and that almost ended my career before it had even begun.

One evening, me and a mate decided to do a bit of night fishing. It was 9:45pm and mum had given us a couple of quid to go to the chippy. The problem was that the chip shop was a mile and a half away and it shut at 10pm so we had to run if we wanted to get some supper. We started jogging and a police car flew past us with the sirens blaring and blue light flashing. We got to within 100 yards of the chippy – I could practically taste the chips – when a policeman came over and asked us why we were running.

"We're getting some chips," I replied. All of a sudden, the handcuffs came out, we were read our rights and we then chucked into the back of the police car.

"What's going on?" I asked.

"We are arresting you for attempted burglary," they replied. Apparently a portacabin that was located between my house and the chip shop had been broken into and they thought that we'd done it. We were shocked.

We were driven to the police station and I was allowed to make a phone call. I rang mum and she soon arrived with my Uncle Charlie and they went mad at me.

"What have you done?" mum yelled. "You know this is going to mess up your football, don't you?"

"Mum, we haven't done anything," I pleaded, but that didn't matter to mum. We were interviewed individually two or three times and the police were really sneaky. They were trying to persuade me to put the blame on my mate. I later found out that they were telling him to say it was me who had done it! They just wanted to solve the case by fitting us up. We were put into seperate cells and left to stew overnight. I was a 14-year-old kid and I don't mind admitting that it was terrifying!

Even though I was innocent, it was still a huge wake up call. While I sat in that cold, dark cell, alone with my thoughts, I realised that I needed to change my ways and behave because my reputation could land me in trouble. All I wanted to do was play football and I knew that I had to grow up, buck my ideas up and keep out of trouble if I wanted to actually make it. If I couldn't be a footballer, my only other option would be to work on the land because that's all I knew and I didn't want to do that. My arrest turned out to be a good lesson for me to learn.

Fortunately, my mate and I were both released without charge the following morning because there was no evidence. Well, of course there wasn't any evidence because we hadn't done anything wrong. Leicester City never found out about my run in with the law, thankfully.

CHAPTER 2
Becoming a Fox

Introduction by Ian Blyth. Former Leicester City teammate.

"The first time that I played against Julian was when we were 13 and I just remember him being strong and very quick. A year later, we joined up together at the Leicester City School of Excellence and we clicked straight away. We had the same sense of humour and we became best pals almost immediately.

While we were in the youth team we got up to all kinds of mischief. Julian's job was to make the tea and he got a lot of stick from the pros, so one day we decided to play a little joke on them. I can't remember whose idea it was – probably mine – but we decided to switch over the sugar and the salt. We looked on as the first teamers poured salt into their drinks. They weren't impressed, but Julian and I thought it was hilarious.

But then the prank went a bit pear shaped. The gaffer, Brian Little, made himself a beef sandwich and he sprinkled what he thought was salt in the middle of his sandwich. I can still picture his face as he politely spat out his sugar-coated beef sandwich and proceeded to blame one of the first teamers who had been dropped the week before! The poor guy protested his innocence, so Steve Hunt, one of the coaches, quizzed the entire youth team in the dressing room about the salt and sugar switch. I'd already warned Jockey not to say anything and we didn't. No one knew it was us – until now!

When he first joined Leicester he took a bit of stick from the lads because of his accent which made him sound like farmer – but that was nothing compared to the hammering that he got when he treated himself to a new jacket with one of his first pay checks.

Julian turned up for training one day in an 8-ball jacket – a suede jacket with a big number eight on the back – thinking that he looked a million dollars. It was a shocker! We hammered him when he wore that that jacket, coupled with his mustard-coloured trousers.

Jockey was a fantastic talent, who could strike the ball like a rocket. Youth team players were getting destroyed by him and it was a no brainer when he eventually moved up to the first team. Julian was a great player and is still a great mate."

*****

I enjoyed the football at the Leicester's School of Excellence, but I found it difficult to settle in because I didn't really know anyone. I couldn't train during term time, so I missed out on a lot of the bonding. Most of the boys there lived in Leicester or Leicestershire and they had different term dates to me which made it even harder. The one person that I did know was Terry Madigan, a mate from Boston who was also in the School of Excellence, and his mum used to drive us the hour and a half to and from training and matches.

In 1991, as I approached my final year of school, my dad asked me what I wanted to do with my life. He laughed when I told him that I wanted to be a footballer. He knew that I was at Leicester, but he was also aware of how tough it was to make the grade, as only a small percentage of players do. He was only trying to look out for me, but he'd never seen me play and didn't know how good I was. There was no alternative for me. I didn't need a back-up plan because I knew that I was going to be a footballer.

Football is a game of fine margins. When I was in the last year of schoolboy forms, the coaches were keeping a close eye on all of us as they had to decide who would be offered a youth contract and who would be released. I didn't know it at the time, but Leicester weren't planning to offer me a contract.

I played mainly as a right winger for City schoolboys, but towards the end of the season, we suffered a few injuries and I was moved to centre forward. I scored a hat-trick in my first game there and the coaches kept me up front for the rest of the season. That was the big turning point for me as I continued to score goals and earnt myself a youth training scheme (YTS) contract. I was one step closer to achieving my dream.

As soon as I signed my YTS apprenticeship contract I thought that I'd made it. I was so excited and couldn't wait to get started, although I knew that I had a lot of growing up to do. I was only 16, a bit naïve and childish and I had to try and find my place in a whole new world.

In July 1991, I packed my bags and with a tinge of sadness, left home and moved 75 miles away to live with people that I didn't know in a brand new city. I moved in with Mr and Mrs Geddes, a lovely couple, in their house on Aylestone Road, Leicester, which was within walking distance of Leicester City's training ground at Belvoir Drive. There were around ten other YTS lads also living there which was a big culture shock for me – I was used to being the only child in my house and I had to get used to sharing a room with three other boys. The house was cramped and you had to fight to get a seat on the sofa in the living room in the evenings.

As you'd expect from a group 16 and 17 year-old lads living away from home for the first time, there was a lot of laughing and joking, but we were all well behaved and I'd been brought up to respect other people and their homes. Discipline was drilled into us from day one; Mr and Mrs Geddes were quite strict and had lots of rules, including a curfew. If you misbehaved, you were reported to the club and no one wanted that.

As a YTS apprentice, I got two free pairs of Gola boots – moulded and stud – from the PFA – so no more stumbling on a hard pitch for me. My wages were £29.50 a week for the first year, rising to £35 in the second – a fortune for me in those days. But the club made me work hard for my money.

It's changed now, but in those days, the youth team players had to do chores and clean the pros' boots. I drew the short straw and got the management team – Brian Little, Allan Evans, John Gregory, and my youth team coaches, David Nish and Steve Hunt. I was desperate to impress them, so I always made sure that their boots were spit shine clean. At Christmas time my teammates were telling me how much the pros had been tipping them – £100 some of them got – but I got nowhere near that because the coaches were a bit tight!

There were other menial jobs that we were expected to do. In the mornings I made the tea, coffee and toast for the coaches before cleaning the big and little gyms. On occasion, I even had to scrub the toilets in the changing rooms – that was probably the worst job. It was a different world to how it is now in academies where the youth teamers are treated like experienced professionals, but I didn't mind it at all and saw it all as part of my development.

The training was a big step up too. I was used to going to school in the day and training once a week, but as a YTS I trained twice a day and did my chores in between. By the time I got back to the digs I was exhausted. It was an incredibly demanding job. But the hard work paid off almost immediately; my fitness went through the roof, I lost pretty much any body fat that I had been carrying, my weight dropped and I was soon in the best shape of my life. Nish and Hunt were fantastic coaches and really helped with my development.

Officially, I was allowed to go back to Boston every six weeks, but in reality, I went home every two or three weeks as I was homesick and missed my friends and family. It was nice to hook up with my mates where they would tell me about all the girls they had met, the partying and all the other things that they'd been doing. At times, it was hard to hear and there were times when I felt that I was missing out, but I just had to get on with it. I was determined not to let anything get in my way because becoming a pro was my dream and all I had ever wanted to do.

On the pitch, things were going great for me. I was scoring goals for fun and towards the end of that first YTS season, I even played a couple of games for the reserves, full on matches against proper pros. It was tough. Most of the defenders that I came up against had been there and done it and had bags of experience. It was a huge challenge and whilst I did well, I wouldn't say it was easy. It's different now with under 23 football, but in those days, reserve games featured a mix of youngsters and experienced pros coming back from an injury. The defenders were big and strong, and the referees allowed a lot more, but it toughened me up. I didn't fear anyone and just played my natural game.

When Brian Little, the first team manager, felt that one of the YTS lads was getting close to the senior squad, they were invited to travel with the first team; not as part of the match-day squad, but just to be around the players to see what it was all about. I was invited to travel twice towards the end of the 1991/92 season.

I was on tea and coffee duty and I used the experience to take it all in and learn what it was like to be a professional footballer. It made me even hungrier to become part of the squad. In my mind I knew that I had made it, I just had to convince everyone else!

It was the perfect time to be at Leicester. The first team had enjoyed a fantastic season, reaching the play off final to take on Kenny Dalglish's Blackburn Rovers for a place in the newly formed Premier League. Sadly, the YTS lads weren't able to go to Wembley in May 1992 to cheer on the boys as we were competing in a couple of tournaments in Holland. It was the first time that I had ever been abroad and we were warned to behave ourselves because we were representing the football club. It was a good tour; I scored a couple of goals and the experience of playing against European teams definitely helped me. When we arrived back in England and stepped off the ferry, we heard that Leicester had lost the play off final. We were all gutted, but it probably helped me out as I knew that there would have been fewer opportunities for young players to break through to the first team if we had been promoted to the Premier League.

I was delighted with my first year as a footballer; I was the youth team's top scorer, had already made my debut for the reserves and my next goal was to sign a professional contract. It happened much sooner than I expected.

When I returned to Belvoir Drive in July 1992 to begin pre-season training, Brian Little told me that I'd be training with the senior squad as well as the youth team. I was only 17 so it was very unexpected, but the gaffer explained that some of the experienced players, including Steve Walsh and Gary Mills, had told him that they wanted me to be involved.

When the season began in August, I got off to a great start by scoring 10 goals in the first five youth team games and also bagged a couple for the reserves.

After training one Friday, the gaffer called me into his office and pushed some papers towards me and said, "Why don't you take a look that." I had a quick look and realised that he had given me a professional contract. My heart was pounding with excitement as Brian explained, "I'm thinking of playing you in the first team, but I can't do that if you haven't signed a contract as someone else could take you. So, what do you think?"

"I'll take it home and let you know next week," I replied.

Brian was shocked as he'd expected me to sign it immediately. But it was a big thing for me and I wanted to speak to mum and nan first.

I also discussed the contract offer with my City teammate, Ian Blyth, who was the same age as me and had already signed a pro contract. Ian was a promising defender who had attended Lilleshall (the FA's School of Excellence) with players like Sol Campbell and we were good mates. Ian had a look at the contract and suggested that I speak with his dad, Jim, a former Scotland international goalkeeper. I told Jim what I'd been offered and he advised me not to sign it and asked if I wanted him to represent me. I listened to his advice but I was worried that the gaffer would be upset if I brought an agent in, so when Monday came around, I went in to see Brian and we did the deal. I signed a contract for £100 a week basic wage with a £50 appearance fee and a £400 win bonus, a huge increase from the £35 a week that I had been getting. I knew that if I could play a couple of games, I'd be earning half decent money.

It wasn't about the money, though. I just wanted to play professional football and this contract meant that I was another step closer. Mind you, I did try and push it and I asked Brian if I could have a signing on fee. He looked at me, laughed and asked, "What do you know about signing on fees?"

"My mum and nan have had to scrimp and save to help me get this far and it's not been easy for them. I just want to repay them for everything they've done for me over the years," I replied.

Brian smiled and said, "I'll see what I can do." True to his word, I got a £1000 signing on fee a week later.

Not long after my 18th birthday, the gaffer told me that he'd selected me in the first team squad for a home game against Barnsley on 3rd October 1993. I was excited and buzzing, but my mind was playing tricks on me. I remember thinking, yes, I'm involved which is great, but I doubt I'll even get on. I was hoping for the best, but not expecting it.

I was expecting to be a substitute, so I was pretty relaxed when I arrived at Filbert Street ahead of kick off. I sat down in the dressing room and looked around at the experience we had; Colin Gibson and Gary Mills had both won the European Cup, Steve Walsh, Ian

Ormondroyd, David Oldfield and Bobby Davison had top-flight experience and there was me with only a handful of reserve games under my belt. When Brian read out the line up, I found out that I was starting and then it was a whole new ball game. All sorts of things were going through my head and I became aware of the butterflies in my stomach. I wasn't nervous, though, because I was always a confident player, I was just brimming with excitement.

I'll never forget the feeling when I walked out of the tunnel for the first time. Every hair on my body was standing on end and I got an unbelievable buzz. I was used to sitting in the stands, cheering on the lads and suddenly, *I* was one of the lads and fans were cheering for *me*.

The pros were great, telling me to enjoy it, to be positive, direct and to play my normal game. There was no pressure on me at all. It was a wonderful experience and I almost scored in the second half. We were losing 1-0 when Bobby Davison crossed the ball into the penalty area. The ball hit my leg, bounced past the Barnsley defenders and I only had the goalkeeper to beat. I thought, 'I can't believe it. I'm going to score at the kop end on my debut, this is amaz –'

And then Simon Grayson took the ball off my foot and scored himself! We won 2-1 and I think I did alright, although I don't really remember much else from the match. That's not uncommon really because as soon as I stepped onto the pitch my whole body took over and it was like I was on auto pilot. I sometimes look back at old clips and think, 'I didn't know I did that!'

I remember exactly what I did in my next game, though, which was a League Cup tie away at Peterborough, the city of my birth. Dad was sat in the Peterborough end, watching me play for the first time and I was keen to show him what I could do. I did exactly that.

Richard Smith's long throw was flicked on by Ian Ormondroyd, our big striker, and as the ball came down to me, I hit it with my right foot. The goalie saved it, but the ball came back to me and I slotted it into the net for my first ever senior goal. As a striker, it was important to get off the mark early doors and that goal gave me the belief that I belonged at that level.

I scored again in our next game, a 2-0 win away at Birmingham City in the league. In just one week, I'd made my debut, played three games and scored two goals. It was a dream start to my professional career.

I'd been playing football at various levels for as long as I could remember and I wasn't fazed by playing in the first team. I could play in front of thousands in the stadium, knowing that millions more were watching live on TV and it never bothered me. I wasn't affect by the cheering, the singing or even the rare occasions when people booed me. Once I stepped over that white line, I was fine. The pitch was *my* domain and I was always confident. But it was an entirely different matter off the pitch.

My rapid rise to the first team meant that I began to get a bit of attention from the fans and media. I was pretty comfortable with the fans coming up to me in the street for a chat or an autograph. They paid my wages, came to the games to support me and I was always happy to give them my time, it was never a problem for me. It still happens today which is nice. People want to talk to me about football and it brings back some good memories when I am reminded about goals that I scored and games that I played in. I've always appreciated the fans' support, that's what it's all about. The fans are so important as we discovered during Covid.

The media attention was a different matter, though. I was, and still am, a very quiet person and I always preferred to sit in the corner of the dressing room, out of the way and take a back seat. Some of my teammates loved seeing their names in the papers and used to court attention, but that wasn't for me. I just wanted to train, play and go home to my family. I was very shy and shunned the limelight. In fact, I hated it, but I had to do my media obligations.

We didn't have any media training back in those days and I just got thrown straight in at the deep end and had to learn pretty quickly. Things happened so fast for me and when I began to make headlines, people wanted to speak to me. I always tried to get out of it when I could, but sometimes it was unavoidable.

I remember the first television interview that I gave – it was a nightmare and I almost swore live on air.

It was 15th November 1992 and we were playing Sunderland at Roker Park. Leicester were pushing for promotion and Sunderland had been the FA Cup runners up in the previous season, so it was a big game that was being broadcast on ITV. It was the first time that I'd played live on TV. I had a blinder, scoring two goals and being named Man of the Match in a 2-1 victory. I was absolutely buzzing as I walked off the pitch until I was told that ITV wanted to interview me. Brian had also been asked and as I stood next to him, I thought, 'this will be alright, the gaffer will look after me.' He went first, before walking off and leaving me to it. Thanks, Brian!

It didn't go well at all. I was nervous, stumbled over my words and hated every minute of it. The interviewer asked me to talk through my goal and I said, "I hit it hard as f–," and luckily stopped myself before I swore live on TV! "I, erm, just hit it as hard as I could," I said instead.

When I got back to the dressing room the lads were all taking the piss out of me. I was only 18 with just a few games under my belt, so I couldn't really speak up and give anything back. Instead, I tried to laugh it off. It was just banter, but thinking back now, it did affect me at the time, and I've never enjoyed interviews since, especially live ones.

It got so bad that if we had a televised match at the weekend, I would worry about it all week. It wasn't anything to do with the amount of people watching the game, it was the thought of having to do a live interview that bothered me. It got into my head big time and I'd get so wound up the night before and during the build-up. I'd question whether I should play within myself because my biggest fear was scoring a goal or, even worse, being named Man of the Match because then I'd have to do another interview.

But as soon as I entered the pitch, all of those thoughts went out of my mind and I wanted to play well to help the team to win. In those days, you couldn't really talk to anyone about things like this, you just had to get on with it. Even when I became an established player, I hated interviews and I think it all stems back to that first one at Sunderland.

Interviews aside, I was flying during my first season as a pro and things got even better on 20th January 1993 when we played Barnsley away in the FA Cup third round replay and I scored the best goal of my career.

I remember Steve Thompson won the ball just outside our penalty area and passed to me on the right-hand side. I was still in my own half with no one ahead of me so I just ran with it until I saw a Barnsley defender coming towards me. I was 25 yards out and thought about going outside and getting a cross in but I decided to shoot instead. I hit it with the outside of my right foot, which was something I used to do a lot in training, and the ball just flew into the top corner. That strike won the Goal of the Month award and was voted the second best Goal of the Season. We lost the tie on a penalty shootout, but no one remembers that, just my goal.

First team football was obviously a lot tougher than I was used to, but I played to my strengths, without fear, and I was absolutely flying. When I had signed my pro contract back in September, Brian told me that when I'd played 20 games, he would rip up the contract and give me a 'proper' one.

As soon as I had played my 21st game I was knocking on the gaffer's door and he knew what was coming.

"Gaffer, you said that I could have a new contract after twenty games," I said.

He winked at me and replied, "There are no flies on you, son. Give me a couple of weeks and I'll sort it out." And he did. I went up to £650 a week, a massive increase and a good wage for an 18-year-old. Now I was earning some proper money, it was time to buy my first car. Brian took me to Fosse Cars on the Fosse Road, owned by Graham Hodges and I bought myself a nice little Ford Fiesta.

Brian had always looked after me and, shortly after I signed that contract, he told me that it was time to get an agent. Ever since my debut, I'd been inundated with people approaching me and the phone at my digs was constantly ringing. There are a lot of shady characters who masquerade as agents, so it is really important to get the right one. I eventually signed with Hayden Evans, who also looked after my teammates, Simon Grayson and Mike Whitlow. I stayed with Hayden for the majority of my career.

As well as a new car, I also had to move to a new house. I'd enjoyed my time living with the Mr and Mrs Geddes, who treated me like family, but once you've signed pro forms the club expect you to move out of digs. I was given a bit longer because of my age. There was a lady, Bev, who worked for Leicester City and one or two players had stayed with her in the past, so I moved into hers for a bit before I found my own place in Markfield, Leicestershire.

Things were getting better and better for me and in February 1993 I received a call up for the World Youth Cup in Australia. My career was going from strength to strength. Twelve months earlier, I hadn't ever been out of England and now I was about to fly to the other side of the world to represent my country!

CHAPTER 3
In the land of Oz

Introduction by Chris Bart-Williams. Member of England's Under 20 squad who competed at the 1993 World Youth Cup.

"*We were full of confidence ahead of the 1993 World Youth Cup in Australia. And why wouldn't we be? We had a very good squad filled with some wonderful characters and fantastic players.*

Initially, the biggest challenge was that our clubs didn't want to release us as the tournament was being held in the middle of the season and many of us were already first team regulars. I was playing for Sheffield Wednesday and we were trying to reach both the FA and League Cup finals.

When we arrived in Australia, we trained pretty damned hard in preparation for the competition. We were competitive, but everyone got on well, strangely enough. Some of us were very loud and boisterous, whereas Julian was super quiet. But when he did speak, his words had a meaning and a presence and I enjoyed speaking and conversing with him throughout the tournament.

Nick Barmby was our first-choice striker, but there was no doubt that Julian was a very good back up.. I'd seen him play on the TV – full games and highlights – and he was quite a talent which is a huge understatement.

Every single player in that squad was a great player, I didn't have any concerns over who was playing. In fact, during one game, I was trying to tell the manager to replace me, because I'd been moved to left midfield, and I felt that there were better players than me in that position. We were that good. When you look back at that squad, most of the lads went on to enjoy long and successful careers.

We definitely practised extremely hard and we played hard in games – that was a given – but on the rare occasions when we had some time off, we socialised hard too. One night, somebody decided that we should go out and see what Melbourne's nightlife had to offer. Usually, I would have declined, but for some reason I went along. There were a number of us who went out and we made sure that we arrived back at the hotel before the curfew. But then we all went back out again! It's one of those rare occasions where we got away with it and the coaches didn't know. At least we didn't think they knew!

It certainly didn't impact upon the practice session the next morning, we made sure of that. We knew that if we were going to burn the candles at both ends, we had to make damn sure that we trained well the following day."

*****

When I made my professional debut, I had achieved one of my dreams. When I was selected to play for England, I fulfilled another.

I was 15, playing in Leicester City's School of Excellence, when I attended a trial for England Schoolboys. There were some good players there, but I did alright and got through to the latter stages, although I was disappointed not to make it any further than that. I was sure that if I kept working hard I would get another opportunity in the future.

It took three years, but I was beyond excited when Brian called me into his office after training one cold February afternoon to tell me that I had been selected for England's squad to compete at the World Youth Cup. I was a bit surprised, though, to be honest as it was an under 20s tournament and I was still only 18 and there were older players with more experience out there. It proved to me that I had been doing something right and it was great to get a call up so early on in my career.

I met up with the squad and the first thing that struck me was that most of the lads were two or three years older than me and some had already played top flight football. The manager, David Burnside, had explained to me that Nick Barmby, who was already playing regularly for Tottenham Hotspurs in the Premier League, was the first-choice striker, but he hoped that I would be involved at some point. I couldn't argue with that and I was just happy to be included and ready to enjoy the experience.

We were a confident bunch and fancied our chances in the tournament as we had a very strong squad, full of talent and most of the lads went on to enjoy good careers in the game. David Watson, Steve Watson, David Unsworth, Ian Pearce, Andy Myers, Chris Bart-Williams, Darren Caskey, Nicky Barmby, Jamie Pollock, Alan Thomson, Andy Johnson, Nicky Butt, Ian Selley and myself, all became established Premier League players. But back then we were just a group of wide-eyed kids, full of excitement for a trip to the other side of the world.

Everything was happening so quickly for me and I didn't have time to think about anything that was going on. I remember turning up at the departure gate at Heathrow and the nerves kicked in as I had never flown before. I didn't really know what to expect and must admit that I was a bit scared as we boarded the plane for the 24-hour flight.

When we landed in Melbourne we were taken to our luxurious hotel before going out for a walk to stretch our legs – long haul flights are not good for young footballers! As we walked around, people were stopping us to say hello and some shouted my name. I was shocked that people on the other side of the world knew who I was as I'd only played a few games by then, none of which had been in the Premier League.

On 7th March 1993, five days after touching down in Australia, we played our first game of the tournament against South Korea. I was an unused substitute as Ian Pearce scored a late equaliser to gain us a valuable point in a 1-1 draw.

I didn't feature in our second group game either, this time against the USA where Chris Bart-Williams' second half strike gave us a 1-0 win. Chris was an unbelievable player who was already playing regularly in the Premier League and his experience was vital for us.

Winning teams only got two points for a win, instead of the usual three, so despite the victory, we still needed to beat Turkey in our final group match to progress to the quarter final.

Nick Barmby was ruled out through injury and Burnside told me that I'd be leading the line. I felt bad for Nick, but these things happen in football and one player's misfortune creates an opportunity for another.

What a feeling it was when I wore the famous three lions' jersey for the first time and stepped onto the pitch at the Olympic Park Stadium in Melbourne. There were almost 13,000 fans in attendance, so the atmosphere was incredible. I felt goosebumps all over my body as we stood and sang the National Anthem.

The excitement was unreal during the build-up, but once the game started, I treated it as just another match. Turkey weren't prepared for my pace and didn't know how to handle me. In the fifth minute, I received the ball and ran at the defence, taking it round two defenders before I was hacked down by a third inside the penalty area. It was a clear penalty, but the referee waved play on. It was frustrating, but I knew I had the beating of them.

A few minutes later, Steve Watson threw the ball into the penalty area and the ball landed kindly for me to smash it home into the back of the net. My first goal for England and a crucial one at that as we went on to win 1-0 to progress to the knockout stages.

Mexico were our opponents in the quarter final and as Barmby was fit again, I was dropped to the bench. The score was 0-0 after extra time and we won 4-3 in a penalty shootout to progress to the semi-final where we would face Ghana. Yes, you read that right - England won a penalty shootout! We knew that we would be in for a tough match as Ghana had won the Under 17 World Cup in 1991 and finished third, earning a bronze medal, in the 1992 Barcelona Olympics.

With Barmby again out injured, I started the match upfront and was marked by a young defender, Sammy Kuffour, who later won the Champions League with Bayern Munich.

It was a tough game and we were 2-0 down at half time. Jamie Pollock netted a spot kick early in the second half to give us a chance, but we just couldn't force an equaliser and we ended up losing 2-1. I was devastated, but there was no time to dwell on the defeat as we still had one final game to play.

The third/fourth place play off is really just a consolation prize for the defeated semi-finalists, but our game was against the hosts, Australia, a country that England have always enjoyed a great sporting rivalry with, so there was a bit more at stake than usual.

There were over 40,000 fans packed into the Sydney Football Stadium – the largest crowd I had played in front of at that stage of my career – and it was a big deal for the Australians who love nothing more than watching their sporting teams beat England. Unfortunately for them, they were in for disappointment.

It was a close match and the score was tied at 1-1 with just five minutes remaining on the clock when Alan Thompson played a stunning long pass that landed straight at my feet. I was on the left-hand side, just outside the Australian penalty area. I had my back to the goal and was aware of two defenders behind me. I turned and sprinted, leaving them in my wake, took it round the goalkeeper and slotted the ball into the empty net to give us a 2-1 win.

Obviously, we wanted to win the tournament, but third place was the best finish that England had ever achieved in the World Youth Cup (until the young lions won it in 2017) and it meant that we were the third best team in the world for our age group. On a personal level, I had gone to the tournament thinking that I'd just be part of the squad and I finished as England's top scorer.

CHAPTER 4
Wembley woes

Introduction by Gary Mills. Former Leicester City captain.

"I made my debut for the championship winning side at Nottingham Forest when I was just 16, so I've always looked out for the young players coming through at all the clubs I've played for. And at Leicester, there was no brighter prospect than Julian Joachim.

Most youngsters struggle to make the step up from the youth team to the professional game, but Julian was the exception. He began training with the first team at the start of the 1992/93 season and it wasn't long before Brian Little gave him his debut. He took it all in his stride, making an instant impact, and he gave us something that we didn't have with his frightening pace.

He was a total threat and with Julian in the side we always felt that we had a chance of scoring goals and winning games. He'd chase and, more often than not, get to the balls that we played over the top or down the right wing because of his speed and he scored some wonderful goals for us. Some very important goals, too.

Julian was a quiet, likeable lad who was great to have around.

Everyone was aware of his pace, but it was his strength that stood out to me, especially considering that he wasn't a big or tall player. He scared our opponents to death."

*****

I returned from Australia with a spring in my step; not only had I demonstrated that I had the ability to perform on the big stage, more importantly, Leicester were enjoying a five-match winning streak and sitting in sixth place in the table, on track to make the play offs.

When the plane landed at Heathrow after the 24 hour journey home, I travelled up to Markfield to drop my bags off and then went straight to Belvoir Drive for training. The gaffer asked me how I felt and I replied that I was raring to go. My confidence was so high that I just wanted to keep playing. So, three days after scoring for England in Sydney, I was back in the starting line-up for City's trip to Cambridge.

I scored the opening goal of the game, although I admit that I had a little bit of luck. I was out wide on the right when I picked the ball up, twisted and turned to beat my defender and then whipped a cross in for Walshy – but it flew into the net instead. Even though I wasn't trying to score, I still claimed it, obviously! Football is like that. When you're playing well and firing on all cylinders, they all seem to go in. It doesn't matter if you scuff it or hit it true, the ball still ends up in the back of the net. We won the game 3-1 so it was a good day all round.

Adrenaline was flowing through my veins and that is how I got through that match. I was a bit jetlagged and halfway through the game, fatigue kicked in and my legs felt really heavy. But I would never refuse the chance to play; that's what I was paid for, that's what I was there to do.

Four days later, 27th March 1993, I again scored the first goal in another 3-1 win, this time over Charlton. In one week, I'd played three games on two different continents and scored three goals.

There was no time to rest as I had received another international call up and made my England Under 18 debut, on 30th March, in a 4-2 win over Denmark. The games were coming rapidly and I was loving it.

My life was like a dream and everything was perfect, until, on 17th April 1993, I received the first red card of my career. We were playing an important match away at Swindon Town. Both clubs were in contention for promotion, so it was a tight, edgy game.

I've always been an easy-going person who tries to avoid conflict. Some opponents had tried to wind me up, but I had never reacted. Even when someone went in late on me deliberately, I was able to control myself. It's not that I was soft, far from it, I had grown up on a council estate and was very streetwise, I just didn't let anyone put me off my game nor did I want to give my opponents the satisfaction of thinking that they'd got to me.

That's why I couldn't believe it when I was sent off for violent conduct – it's just not in my nature.

Kevin Poole, our goalkeeper, was preparing to take a goal kick and I was standing in the centre circle facing the ball. Swindon's big defender, Colin Caulderwood, was standing behind me when he grabbed my throat. There is usually a bit a jostling, but this was too much as I couldn't breathe. The feeling reminded me of the asthma attacks that I used to suffer from when I was a kid. I tried but was unable to get his arms off me and I went into panic mode. I bent forwards and flung him over my shoulder using some kind of judo move. As he tumbled to the ground, he grabbed onto my shirt and it felt like I was being strangled again. When you are struggling to breathe, you just focus on survival, so I moved my arms around four or five times to try and get him to release his hold on my shirt. When I finally felt his grip loosen, I managed to get my breath back. There was nothing malicious in my actions, but the referee saw something different and gave me a yellow card. I couldn't believe it! All I had done was to defend myself.

Then I noticed the linesman had his flag up and the ref. went over to have a word with him. When he returned to the pitch, he told me that the linesman said that I'd thrown punches at Caulderwood and he sent me off! It was the first time that I'd ever been shown a red card at any level. I barely received yellow cards, so it was a huge shock.

I was incensed. If it wasn't for Caulderwood grabbing me in the first place, it wouldn't have happened. I trudged down the tunnel and sat in the dressing room, on my own, for the remainder of the match which we drew 1-1. We'd have preferred the win, but the bigger problem was that my red card meant that I would have to serve a suspension. The gaffer told me not to worry about it and said that the club would submit an appeal.

So a few days later, we travelled down to London for a hearing at the FA headquarters on Lancaster Gate. It was a strange experience, a bit like waiting outside the headmaster's office! Before the hearing, Brian and I were standing in the corridor ready to be called in and meet the panel, when the referee and linesman from the Swindon game walked over to us. The referee said, "I've looked at the replays and wanted to give you a heads up that I'm not changing my mind. In my opinion you deserved the red card."

"We've got to hope that the panel see it differently," Brian told me. It felt like we were up against it before the hearing had even began.

Before long, we were invited into the hearing. Brian and I took our seats next to the linesman and the referee and were introduced to the panel, then we all watched the incident numerous times in slow motion on a large monitor. It was a bit like watching the VAR decisions now.

Brian then stood up and talked through the footage, explaining that I was just defending myself. He'd even taken the shirt that I was wearing with him to show the panel how tight it was.

Then it was the referee's turn. He stood up next to screen, pressed play on the video and explained what was happening, from his point of view. Then he suddenly said, "Oh, I've got it all wrong. Julian didn't punch him."

I was so relieved and it showed a lot about the referee's character that he wasn't afraid to admit that he'd made a mistake. The panel rescinded the red card and afterwards the referee came over to apologise to me which was nice. I never received a red card in my career again.

As I was no longer suspended, I started in our next game on 20th April and bagged a brace in a 4-1 victory over Southend that secured our place in the play offs.

We eventually finished sixth in the league and were drawn against Portsmouth in the two-legged semi-final. We were just two games away from Wembley, but we knew that it wasn't going to be an easy task to get past Pompey who had finished third, narrowly missing out on automatic promotion because of goal difference.

Filbert Street was being redeveloped to increase capacity and the Main Stand had been demolished after our final home game of the season against Bristol City. With Filbert Street unavailable, our play off semi-final 'home' leg was held at the City Ground, Nottingham. It was a very strange experience playing a home game at the ground of our biggest rivals, Nottingham Forest.

I remember that it took forever to get to the ground because of the heavy traffic. Instead of hiring a coach, the players had to make our own way there and most of us were late. It wasn't ideal preparation for such a huge game and when I finally arrived at the City Ground, I found out that the gaffer had decided to go with experience which meant that I was on the substitutes' bench. I was really frustrated because I wanted to play every game, especially the big ones.

I watched the match from the bench and could see that there was little to split the sides, so I was itching to get on as I felt that I could change the game. Eventually, Brian brought me on and before long, I'd scored. It was one of the most memorable and important goals that I ever got. The fans remember it fondly too.

When I got the ball, I just did what I'd been doing since I was a kid. I didn't think, 'I'll do this and that,' I didn't have a clue what I was going to do, it was totally instinctive.

Simon Grayson poked the ball up to me. I was inside my own half and knew that the defender was tight on me, so when I received the ball, I turned him and noticed that there was a lot of space in front of me, so I just ran. As I approached the Portsmouth penalty area, two defenders tried to block my path, but I just knocked it past them, used my pace and went straight for goal. When the ball hit the back of the net the fans went wild and it was a great feeling, especially as it was the winning goal.

We drew the return fixture 2-2, giving us a 3-2 aggregate victory and a place in the play off final. Swindon Town, managed by Glenn Hoddle, were our opponents.

Most of the lads had been involved in the 1992 play off final, but it was all new to me. I wasn't nervous at all, just excited and couldn't wait for the game. It might sound a bit flippant, but in those days so much had happened to me in such a short space of time that I didn't really consider the enormity of the occasion. The games were coming thick and fast, and I was too busy playing football to worry about how big each game was. It was refreshing and helped me to cope. Maybe if I'd actually taken the time to consider what was happening to me, it would have added unnecessary pressure. In those early days I didn't feel any pressure at all. It was just football and I kept my focus on each individual game. All of a sudden, the season had gone and we were in the play off final playing for a place in the Premier League.

The build up to the match was different to normal games. We stayed in a hotel for a couple of days before the game and the hotel staff gave us the special treatment that was usually reserved for VIPs. I remember speaking to my mates back in Leicester and they told me that there was a huge buzz around the city which just increased my levels of excitement.

On the day of the match, we boarded the coach and as we drove up Wembley Way, I caught my first glimpse of the famous stadium, the Twin Towers and the thousands of City fans who'd turned up to line the streets to support us. I'd never even been to Wembley before, as a player or a fan, and the gaffer had already told me that I was going to start. Who would have thought that at the beginning of the season when I was turning out for the youth team?

I knew that it was a special occasion because even my mum was sitting in the stands to cheer me on. It was the first time she had ever seen me play as she wasn't a huge football fan. My uncles had persuaded her to come to Wembley.

As I walked out of the tunnel, we were greeted with a ticker tape reception and I remember the noise emanating from the 73,000 supporters in the stands. It was like nothing that I'd ever experienced before. This was the big time, it was amazing!

But the game didn't go to plan at all. Swindon scored either side of half time and got a third in the 53rd minute. We were 3-0 down with less than half the game remaining. We couldn't believe it and I remember thinking, 'what's going on?' Things were not looking good and I think everyone watching assumed that the game was already over.

But we were a tight-knit group who fought for one another and there was no way that we were going to cave in, although many a team probably would have. We picked ourselves up and had nothing to lose. I remember our defender, Colin Hill, was screaming and shouting at us, "Go out there and give it everything you've got. We can get back into this game."

The fans were behind us, too, which was a massive help and we fought for our lives. Just before the hour mark, Lee Philpott found some space down the left-hand side and whipped in a cross. Steve Walsh's header hit the post and I smashed in the rebound. Inside, I was absolutely buzzing to have scored a goal at Wembley, but there was no time to celebrate because we still needed two more goals. I raised my hand to salute the supporters and rushed back to the centre circle so that we could restart the match as quickly as possible. My goal gave everyone a little lift and ten minutes later, Walshy pulled another one back.

Then, unbelievably, in the 69th minute, our comeback was somplete when Steve Thomson bagged the equaliser. I have never again experienced the feeling I got when Thommo scored. It was such a rollercoaster of emotion. We had the excitement of the pre-match build up, the low of being 3-0 down and then the high of coming back to make it 3-3.

But there was more drama to come.

Just six minutes from time, Swindon were awarded a dubious penalty which they scored. We lost 4-3 and I cannot describe how devastated I felt. We put everything into that game and I was exhausted, both physically and mentally. To lose in that manner was awful for us on the pitch and for those loyal fans in the stands. Being honest, I found it hard to pick myself up after that and felt flat for weeks afterwards.

It was an incredible game, one of the greatest ever Wembley matches, and unfortunately there had to be a loser. When we returned to the dressing room, we could hear the Swindon players celebrating next to us which was horrible, but I was respectful and went over to congratulate them.

I'll never forget that game and although it was tough to swallow at the time, I think it helped to strengthen the character of the team. After two successive play off final defeats, we were determined to be the ones celebrating the following year.

CHAPTER 5
Little Romario

Introduction by Mark Tinkler. Member of England's Under 18 squad who competed in the 1993 European Champtionships.

"It was an unbelievable time for us. We were a group of young lads, representing England in the European Championships which was being held in our own country. The crowds were massive and with most of the games televised live on Sky Sports, we felt that we had the backing of the whole country. It was a fantastic time and something that I'll never forget. I think that goes for all the players involved, even those who went on to have great careers, I don't think they'll ever forgot what we achieved that summer.

I was one of five Leeds players in the squad and there were three lads from Manchester United. There was quite a lot of rivalry between the two teams; United won the Premier League in 1993 and Leeds had won it the season before. United had won the FA Youth cup in 1992 and we beat them to win it in 1993. So, as you can imagine, there was quite a lot of banter flying about between us Leeds lads and Butty, Scholesy and Nev of Manchester United.

But we put that rivalry aside when we joined up for England duty. There was obviously a bit of craic, and we'd wind the United lads up at times, but it was all good-natured fun. There was a lot of confidence in the England camp and we were all focussed on doing as well as we could for our country.

We all knew about Julian and had seen how well he was doing at the time. A few of us had made our first team debuts during the 1992/93 season, but Julian had played a lot more games than most of us, so we were aware of how talented he was. He was kind of a quiet lad, but everyone loved him. A few other lads were quite *quiet and reserved, but we all got to know each other well as the tournament progressed, and we enjoyed some mickey taking and the normal laughs you get with a group of 17 and 18 year olds!*

Julian was a real talent; electric pace that frightened defenders, powerful, very dynamic, had great skill and was a quality finisher. He was a real asset for England during that competition. He was a good outlet for us as a team with the runs he made behind the back four. If he was in a position where he was one-on-one, we knew he was likely to go past the defender and either get a shot on target or create a chance for someone else. He was fantastic in that tournament and a big factor in our success."

*****

There was little time to dwell on the Wembley defeat as I was due to meet up with the England Under 18 squad ahead of the UEFA Under 18 European Championships that were being held in England during the summer of 1993.

Our manager, Ted Powell, had selected an initial squad of 25 lads that had to be whittled down to 16 by the time the tournament kicked off. Having played for the age group above earlier in the season and with a full season of first team football under my belt, I was confident that I'd be one of the lucky 16, but it wasn't a given and I had to work hard in training and try to impress the manager.

I didn't know many of the players as most members of the squad hadn't played a lot of first team football and as I didn't play many games for the reserves, our paths hadn't really crossed before. But some of my teammates had already began to garner reputations; mainly the lads from Manchester United and Leeds who had won the 1992 and 1993 FA Youth Cups respectively.

During training, I instantly saw that there was so much quality within the squad. Even though we were a bunch of unproven youngsters, these boys were on a different level to the young lads at Leicester. I don't mean any disrespect by that at all. Most youngsters have something that they excel at - passing, tackling, finishing, etc. – these guys had the lot.

To give you an idea of the quality that we had, David Beckham, who was named in the initial 25-man squad, didn't make the final cut. He was a year younger than a lot of us and he was very unlucky, but his time obviously came later. It was clear that he was a quality player, but I had no idea that he would go on to have the career that he did. It was Paul Scholes, Sol Campbell, Nicky Butt and Gary Neville who looked the real deal at that age.

Ted Powell kept cutting back the squad and before we knew it, there were just 16 of us remaining: Chris Day (Spurs), Andy Marshall (Norwich), Gary Neville (Manchester United), Sol Campbell (Spurs), Chris Casper (Manchester United), Kevin Sharp (Leeds), Rob Bowman (Leeds), Darren Caskey (Spurs), Mark Tinkler (Leeds), Nicky Butt (Manchester United), Paul Scholes (Manchester United), Jamie Forrester (Leeds), Noel Whelan (Leeds), Kevin Gallen (QPR), Robbie Fowler (Liverpool) and me – a hugely talented group, hungry for success. We knew that we had a chance, especially as we had the home advantage.

I have since heard stories of cliques within international setups, but there was none of that with the Under 18s, despite some playing for rival clubs. We all got on well and enjoyed a few laughs, although there was no messing about. In club football, there are little routines or initiations. For example, if you're the worst trainer you might have to sing a song or drive an old banger for a week, but there was nothing like that at England. It was much more serious because we were only together for a short period of time and we were 100% focussed on winning the tournament.

We had the ability, the confidence and the fans behind us, but we knew it wasn't going to be an easy task. We were in a very tough group with France, Holland and Spain and the format meant that only one team from each group would progress to the final.

We got off to a great start, beating France 2-0 in our opening match which was held at Stoke City's Victoria Ground. Powell set us up in an attacking formation with Kevin Gallen, Robbie Fowler and myself leading the line. Gallen and Fowler scored our goals.

In our second match, we came up against a very strong Dutch side featuring Patrick Kluivert, Giovanni Van Bronckhorst and Clarence Seedorf, who had already made his debut for Ajax. They were the tournament favourites and everyone expected them to beat us convincingly. Everyone but us, that is.

We played some fantastic football and Holland just couldn't cope with our pace and attacking style. It was one of those games where individually and collectively we were superb and no one put a foot wrong. Fowler and Gallen bagged a goal apiece, and I got the other two – both with my left foot which was rare.

My second goal was the best of the two. Darren Caskey chipped the ball over to me in the Dutch penalty area. One of their defenders closed in tight which meant that I didn't have enough room to turn, so I flicked it over his head with my right foot, spun around and volleyed the ball home with my left. It was all instinctive and was one of the best goals that I ever scored.

We were all buzzing after the match. Two wins from two but it would mean nothing if we failed to beat Spain who had also won their opening two matches.

The first half was very tense with Spain dominating possession, displaying the passing style that they later became famous for. We kept going, defended strongly and maintained our shape, knowing that we'd eventually break them down. Against the run of play, Mark Tinkler gave us the lead just on the stroke of half time. At the break, Powell instructed us to be more attacking and take the game to Spain. There was no talk of sitting back and defending our slender lead because we were so strong going forward. Attack was our first form of defence.

They equalised in the seventieth minute and then, just like in the game against Holland, everything just clicked. Fowler bagged a hat trick and Jamie Forrester scored our fifth to give us a 5-1 victory. To put five past a team like Spain was incredible. Our mentality was to play attacking football with the aim of outscoring our opponents. We could score goals throughout the team – Fowler in particular was a superb finisher. He was an incredible player, even at that age. A natural goal scorer, who could score all kinds of goals and made it all look so easy. It was obvious to anyone who watched him during that tournament that Robbie was going to be a top player.

We didn't really have to worry about conceding as we were blessed with a strong defence, including Gary Neville and big Sol Campbell.

Sol was a giant for his age – a real man mountain. He'd already made his Premier League debut for Spurs by then. He was strong but also quick once he got into his stride. What is amazing is that he started out as a striker before he became one of the best defenders of his generation.

On 25th July 1993, we took on Turkey, the holders, in the tournament final, which was held at the City Ground, Nottingham. It is amazing that two of the biggest matches of my short career took place at the home of Leicester's biggest rivals. There were almost 24,000 fans inside the stadium and the match was broadcast live on Sky Sports. I think the supporters were expecting another goal fest, but the final was very tight and cagey, with neither team wanting to lose. I had a few chances that were well saved by the 'keeper and the match was deadlocked until the 77th minute.

I picked up the ball just inside the opponents' half and did what I do best – ran at the defence. I twisted and turned past two defenders and used my pace to accelerate away from them. I had the goal in my sight when I was taken clean out just before I had a chance to shoot. The referee gave us a penalty which Darren Caskey, our captain, put away. We held on to win the game and the tournament. It was an amazing feeling when the ref blew the full-time whistle and we celebrated on the pitch before being presented with the trophy.

It had been an incredible first season for me and this really was the icing on the cake. After the disappointment of the semi-final defeat in the World Youth Cup back in March and the devastation of the play off final in May, it was nice to finally get a winners' medal.

There was more good news for me on a personal level. My second goal against Holland was awarded Goal of the Tournament and I was named Player of the Tournament – it was like a dream!

There were a lot of people comparing my style of play to the Brazilian striker Romario, with one newspaper giving me the nickname 'Little Romario'. What a great player he was. A small striker, like me, I used to watch him on the TV a lot to study his movement, positioning and the runs that he made. It was unbelievable to hear my name mentioned in the same breath as his.

We all like to hear good things said about us and I was no different. I bought all the newspapers that I could find, just to keep reading the kind things that people were saying about me. Although, my feet were firmly on the ground and I didn't get carried away at all – Brian wouldn't have let me. Looking back now, I probably should have spent some time appreciating what was going on and what I had accomplished, but instead my mind was always on the next game. It was a great start to my football career, but there was still a lot more that I wanted to achieve. This was just the beginning.

CHAPTER 6
Premier League dreams

Introduction by Bobby Davison. ***Former Leicester City Striker***

"Julian was taking his first steps in what would become a successful football career when I first met him. I could see straight away that this boy was going to be something special. A quiet man, built like an international sprinter, Julian was an outstanding young talent.

I was approaching the end of my career and I gave Julian little snippets of things that I had learned over the years, like how to time his runs. I passed on my knowledge, but it was up to Julian to put it into practice, and it's made my day to hear that he feels I helped him.

I enjoyed playing alongside Julian, watching him tear defenders apart. It is the striker's job to put the defence under pressure and to make it hard for them. And that's exactly what Julian did. You ask any defender who played against him and they will tell you that he was a nightmare. He had everything; pace, technique, fantastic dribbling and exceptional finishing. He could play on the left, right or even as a number ten role.

Julian reminded me a little of Gary Speed, who had broken into the first team while I was at Leeds United. Both were very talented players and both were shy lads who avoided the limelight. But come match day, they were able to turn it on and make you go 'wow.'

Julian stormed onto the scene but didn't let it go to his head. He must have been a manager's dream as he was never flash and had a top-notch attitude.

If he was playing today, he would be up there with the best. When I look at some of the young players who are in the England squad today, Julian would easily hold his own."

*****

The gaffer gave me a two-week break to recover from the international tournament and then I was straight back into it. I was already match fit and didn't want too much time off because I was worried that I'd lose my sharpness and a bit of fitness, so a fortnight off was ideal. There wasn't really any time for rest anyway, as the new season was only a few weeks away, and although I probably was tired, I didn't notice it because I was buzzing from playing so much football and the adrenaline was getting me through it. It had obviously been a gruelling season with two international tournaments, but I was raring to go and desperate to join up with the lads and resume training.

I had scored 13 goals in my first season for Leicester and there were lots of rumours in the newpapers of the various clubs who were interested in me. Arsenal and Blackburn were two Premier League sides that I was linked with. I was flattered, but I wanted to stay at Leicester and didn't even ask the club if they had received any offers. Brian made it clear to me and the fans that I wasn't for sale and he even told the press that he would resign if the club sold me. That was a huge thing for him to say and showed how highly he rated me. When your manager is saying things like that, why would I want to leave?

I was also in demand from sponsors and my agent managed to negotiate a couple of really good deals for me. Puma became my boot sponsors and as well as supplying me with as many pairs of Puma Kings (*the* boots to have at the time) as I needed, I could also choose whatever Puma gear I needed, and they would deliver it to my front door the next day. In those days I was always in tracksuits, so it was ideal. Oh, and they also gave me a couple of quid too.

The other deal that my agent arranged was with Sytner's BMW, who gave me a free BMW 316i to drive! It was a fantastic car that I fell in love with straight away. The perks of being a footballer! I had only passed my driving test 12-months earlier.

We knew that we were already close to promotion, having been play off finalists the previous two years, but we needed a couple of new faces to strengthen the squad. The gaffer bought in goalkeeper, Gavin Ward and defender Brian Carey, two solid players but it was his third signing that shocked everyone.

In the 1992 play off final, David Speedie had gone down in the penalty area after minimal contact from Steve Walsh. Mike Newell scored the resulting spot kick which won Blackburn a place in the inaugural Premier League at Leicester's expense. The City fans and a lot of our players felt that Speedie had dived, so to say he wasn't very popular in Leicester is a huge understatement. Which is why no one could believe it when Brian turned up at Belvoir Drive accompanied by Speedie and introduced him to the lads as our new signing!

It was a really weird situation because no one wanted him at the club - not the players nor the fans. I remember that Walshy, in particular, wasn't happy and went to speak to Brian about it. It said a lot about Speedie's character that he was prepared to join us and to help us in our promotion bid despite knowing the welcome that he was likely to receive. During his first training session, he took a lot of stick from the lads and there were one or two crunching tackles flying around, but once we saw what he could bring to the team, especially his goalscoring ability, we knew that he'd be an asset and we gave him a chance. And what a signing he turned out to be!

Secretly, I was delighted that he'd joined us because I was a young lad still learning my trade and he spent a lot of time helping me. Speedie had bags of experience having played for Liverpool, Chelsea and a host of other top clubs during a lengthy career. He was a small striker, like me, and became a mentor to me, helping to improve my movement and positioning. Speedie and Bobby Davison were my two favourite strike partners while I was at Leicester.

When Speedie made his debut against Peterborough on 14th August 1994, the Foxes fans didn't know whether to cheer for him or boo him, but four goals in his first six games showed everyone just what he could offer and as soon as the supporters saw how committed he was to our cause, he was forgiven. Leicester fans like to see the lads play with passion and determination and that was what Speedie brought to the team.

Ok, so he dived in the play off final, but being honest, if he was playing for us in that game and had won the penalty that sent us up, I'm sure we'd have all been cheering for him.

I think that if they're honest with themselves, most strikers will admit that they have exaggerated contact and gone down easily at least once in their career. If you get hit in the box, eight times out of ten you're going to go down. I was probably too honest and tried to stay up if I was in a goal scoring position because I didn't take the penalties and wanted to score myself. There were a few times where I was fouled, tried to stay up, couldn't and didn't get the penalty, so it makes you think twice next time. Occasionally, I did go to ground if I'd been touched, even if it was slight contact, but it was never anything blatant. I never deliberately tried to con the ref and I never went down without contact. That's not in my nature and I see diving as a form of cheating. There is way too much of it now and it's ruining the game.

I think a few people expected us to struggle after the devastating defeat to Swindon, but we proved them wrong. By mid-September, we moved up to sixth place in the league table and we remained in the top six for the remainder of the season. The day after a game, I would read the tabloids to see what had been said about me and to have a look at the league table. That's a lot easier to do when you're playing well and winning games. I hated losing. When we did lose a game, I would be distraught, and my weekend would be ruined, but once I returned to training the defeat had been forgotten.

The reason that we were able to pick ourselves up so well is because of the fantastic team spirit that we enjoyed. We had a real family feel around the club, especially in the dressing room. If we had a night out (of which there were many!) around 15-20 of the lads would turn up and we always had a great time. It wasn't like that at any other club that I played for, you might have five or six turn up, but never the whole squad. The nights out were good social occasions, but they also helped us to bond and to create the good team spirit for which Leicester was renowned.

Walshy was the skipper and a proper leader. He commanded so much respect from his teammates that we used to call him 'Mr Leicester'. He'd run through brick walls for City, and we knew that he always had our backs, on and off the pitch. He treated every game like he was going to war and the opposing forwards always knew that they'd been in a game when they played against him. I played up front with him during the 1992/93 season and we perfected the big man/little man routine and scored a lot of goals between us. Walshy loved a night out with the lads too.

Bobby Davison was another striker that I enjoyed playing alongside. He was an experienced pro, coming to the end of his career when he joined us, while I was at the start of my journey. Everything I did was off the cuff, and he put me right on a few things, teaching me when and when not to make runs.

Simon 'Larry' Grayson was another good lad. He was so versatile and could play centre back, right back or even in midfield. He was a very underrated player who enjoyed a fantastic career. With Gary Mills injured, he took the captains' armband towards the end of the 1993/94 season and, like Millsy, he was an inspirational leader.

Steve Thompson was a class act in midfield. He was fantastic in dead ball situations and scored some wonderful goals for us. I got on really well with him off the pitch too, as we both shared an interest in horse racing. Thomo was another who enjoyed the social events with the boys.

My best friend at the club was Ian Blyth. A Burbage lad the same age as me, Ian was highly regarded in football and, as I have mentioned earlier, he had been at Lilleshall (the National School of Excellence) along with my England under 18 teammate, Sol Campbell. People expected big things of Ian who was considered to be the brightest young prospect that Leicester had. He signed pro forms before I did, but he suffered a lot of injuries and was forced to move down the leagues, so he never got the opportunity to fully reach his potential. Ian is still my best friend today.

Back to football and at the end of October, we had a chance to test ourselves against the very best in the country when we were drawn to play the Premier League Champions, Manchester United, in the third round of the League Cup. We were fourth in the league table at the time and felt optimistic about our promotion chances and I remember thinking that the game against United would be a good way of measuring where we were.

We lost 5-1 which was a real eye opener. It showed us that we were a long way off where we needed to be if we wanted to compete with the best clubs around. Looking back now, we weren't the most talented team, but what we did have was fight, determination and a whole lot of togetherness. You could see that by the way we came together on the pitch; it was like going to war and we'd all fight for our teammates. We knew that we needed more than that for the Premier League and it would be a steep learning curve for us. Saying that, we weren't the only team who got turned over at Old Trafford in those days.

We bounced back well though and two weeks after the United game we moved to the top of the league following a 3-0 win over Southend at Filbert Street.

At the end of November, the gaffer dipped into the transfer market to sign Iwan Roberts from Huddersfield. Iwan was a prolific goal scorer and was exactly the kind of player that we needed to replace Steve Walsh, our top scorer from the previous year, who had suffered a cruciate ligament injury earlier in the season. Iwan partnered Speedie up front and I was moved out to the wing.

I preferred playing as a striker, but I didn't mind playing out wide on the right when the team needed me to. I found it was harder to play as a winger because there was a lot of work involved. My strengths were getting forward and causing problems for the opponents with my pace, but as a winger I was expected to get back and support with the defensive side, something that I've never been great at. I tried, of course, but it zapped my energy so much that when we were attacking, I struggled to find my usual burst of pace to get away from defenders as I was exhausted. I felt like I was in an impossible situation; Gary Mills was often our right back and he'd be telling me to get back into position and support him defensively, while I'd have the strikers in my other ear telling me to stay forward and save my energy for our attacks. In my first 18 months as a professional, I'd played so much football that my body was beginning to feel weary. After about an hour of each game, I'd get leggy and start to cramp up.

It wasn't just the physical exertion that was tiring me out. Football is mentally exhausting, too, and you have to be exceptionally strong in your mind. People often think that football is easy, that it's just running around for an hour and a half each week, but in some ways the mental side can be harder. I've seen very talented lads, players who you think are certain to make it, fall out of the game because they lacked the mental strength and couldn't handle the pressure. It's not all about your skill or physical attributes; you have to be fully committed and it has to mean everything to you. I had to sacrifice a hell of a lot and not everyone is prepared to do that.

In my early days, I found the build up to a game was very draining. I'd train all week and then come Friday night, my focus turned to the game on the following day. I used to visualise it, think about what I was going to do, who I was going to be up against and play through various scenarios in my head. I wouldn't think of anything other than the upcoming match. It took a lot of out me and as I became more experienced, I learnt to switch off and conserve my energy for the actual game.

These are the kind of things that you learn over time, but it really helps to have a good manager who knows how to treat and advise players as individuals. You get the shouters and ballers and some players need that. Not me. With my character I much preferred a manager who adopted a quieter approach. I was always clear on what was expected of me before I went onto the pitch and by half time I knew what sort of game I was having. If I hadn't played well, I'd half give myself a bollocking, I didn't need anyone else to do it. If things had gone well, I'd just keep it going with more of the same. Brian was the perfect manager for me. He had an air of authority about him, gave clear simple instructions and didn't raise his voice a lot. Mind you, he wasn't afraid to discipline us when he felt it was appropriate, he just preferred to deal with things in private as I discovered in December 1993.

We were playing away at Southend, which was a 170-mile round trip, so we travelled down the day before the game and stayed overnight in a hotel. I was rooming with Steve Thompson and on the morning of the match, as we returned to our rooms after breakfast, we were told that lunch was being served at noon and that we'd be leaving the hotel to travel to the ground at 1.30 p.m. Neither Steve nor I ate a pre-match meal, so we decided to skip lunch and meet the rest of the lads in reception just before we were due to leave.

At 1 p.m. we were lying on our beds watching TV and having a chat when there was a knock at the door. It was Taff Davies, the kitman, telling us to hurry up because the coach was ready to leave. Brian had decided to get to the ground a little earlier and had told the lads at lunch, but no one had thought to tell us!

We quickly got changed, packed our bags and left the hotel. As we boarded the coach and walked past the gaffer, I was expecting him to ask where we'd been, but he didn't say a word. He didn't even make eye contact with us and it was obvious that he wasn't happy. As we walked down the coach, the other lads were giving us a look that told us that we were in trouble.

We arrived at Roots Hall, got to the dressing room and then Brian read out the team for the match – Gavin Ward in goal. Mike Whitlow, Brian Carey, Simon Grayson and Neil Lewis at the back. Steve Agnew, Gary Mills, Lee Philpott and Steve Thompson in midfield and Iwan Roberts and David Speedie upfront. My name was missing. Not just from the starting line up, I didn't even make the bench. I'd been involved in the last 12 games, starting nine and I felt angry that I'd been dropped for something that wasn't my fault. Thomo still played, so I felt that I was being treated unfairly. I had to watch from the stands as we drew the game 0-0. Maybe I'd have made the difference, but who knows?

Brian called me in to his office the following Monday. "That's the first fucking time I've been pissed off with you," he told me. He had never sworn at me before and I felt like I was in the headmaster's office when he told me off! It was Brian's way of keeping my feet on the ground and he dealt with it in the right way by discreetly telling me off, rather than giving me a bollocking in front of everyone else. He didn't hold a grudge and I was back in the starting line-up for our next game. I felt that I had a point to prove and I scored three goals in the next six games. And I was never late again in my career.

In January 1994, we had another chance to test ourselves against Premier League opposition when we travelled to Manchester again, this time to face Manchester City at Maine Road in the third round of the FA Cup. It was another rout and we lost 4-1. It was a tough defeat to take as we'd been winning regularly in the league and then went and suffered such a heavy loss. We were outclassed, but it was another good lesson for us to learn and another reminder of where we needed to be if we did win promotion.

We put the FA Cup setback aside to beat Charlton 2-1 which sent us back to the top of the league. It was very tight at the top of the table, but we felt that we could kick on and gain automatic promotion.

On the 8th March 1994, I made my England Under 21 debut in a 1-0 win over Denmark. I came on as a substitute for Nick

Barmby to achieve another milestone in my career, but I can't really remember too much from the game.

When I returned to Leicester, we had dropped to second place, still in the hunt for an automatic promotion slot, but then we had an awful run of results where we won just twice in the final twelve games. I can't really put my finger on why we struggled to win. It's not as if we were playing poorly as we only lost three times, we just weren't clinical enough to finish teams off which is why we drew seven matches. It was a disappointing end to the season, but we still managed to finish fourth which meant that we had qualified for the play offs.

We drew (again!) in the first leg against Tranmere Rovers, before beating them 2-1 at Filbert Street which meant that we progressed to the final. It was fitting that it was David Speedie who scored the winning goal, finally earning forgiveness from the City fans. He received a red card shortly after scoring which meant that he would miss the final.

So, we were in the play off final for the third time in three years and although we had the experience our opponents, Derby County, were the big favourites. They had spent huge sums of money on assembling an exceptionally talented squad, with lots of individuals who later played in the Premier League. There was a great rivalry between the two clubs and that all added to the occasion.

When we arrived at Wembley, I found out that I was on the bench as the gaffer had decided to go with a big, strong side to try and bully the opposition. The strikers that he picked were all over six feet tall; Ian Ormondroyd, Iwan Roberts and Steve Walsh, who had only just returned from injury and needed an injection to play.

I was obviously disappointed not to start, but I knew the gaffer had a game plan and I trusted him. At least I was still involved and I felt confident that I'd come on at some stage during the match.

Derby scored early doors through Tommy Johnson (who later became a teammate of mine) and they created a hatful of chances that their strikers failed to put away. Walshy equalised for us just before half time to put us back in the game. Derby dominated the second half and we rode our luck a few times.

I finally came on in the 56th minute to replace Iwan Roberts and it was good to get on. As I crossed the touchline on to the hallowed turf, I remembered how I had felt at the end of the last match I played at Wembley, our 4-3 defeat to Swindon, and was determined not to experience that devastation again.

With just five minutes left on the clock, I received the ball with my back to the Derby goal. I could see Simon Grayson making a run down the right-hand side, so I played a through ball to him. Larry whipped in a cross, Ormondroyd's header was saved and Walshy was there to bury the rebound. What a feeling that was. Relief, happiness and also some nerves because the game wasn't over just yet – a whole mixture of emotions.

Derby were shellshocked - just as we had been 12 months earlier - and we held on to win 2-1. It was City's first ever victory at Wembley. When the referee blew the final whistle, I jumped for joy, it was an incredible feeling. Finally, I was going to have the opportunity to test myself against the best defenders in the land. I remember the noise from the fans was deafening as we climbed the famous steps to receive our winners' medals, the play off trophy and, more importantly, a place in the Premier League.

CHAPTER 7
A family man

During the summer of 1994, I had my first proper break since turning pro and I spent it with my girlfriend, Kate, and her two kids.

I had first met Kate when I had been living in digs on Aylestone Road. Kate lived in a nearby street and I remember seeing her in the local shop from time to time. She was a knockout and I knew instantly that I liked her, but I was a shy lad, so I didn't say anything to her until a while later when I saw her in a nightclub in Leicester. She was there with my cousin who introduced us and we got talking and swapped numbers at the end of the night. It didn't bother me that Kate was a few years older than me and that she had two kids from previous relationships. I'd not long come out of a semi-serious relationship myself and wasn't looking for anything too serious, so we agreed to take it slow. We just sort of went out a few times to have some fun and to see what happened. We went from strength to strength and before long, Kate and her two children, Jadine, aged six, and Roche, aged one, had moved in with me.

I suppose that a lot of people my age wouldn't have wanted to settle down with a ready-made family, but I enjoyed being a family man. It calmed me down a bit and stopped me partying all the time, so Brian was pleased too.

I realised early on that there was a lot responsibility attached to being a family man. Like most young men, I liked a drink and a night out with the lads, but I knew my limits and was never a big drinker. I'd get tipsy, but no more than that as I knew that the next morning, I would have kids to play with and there would be nappies to change – and it's certainly no fun doing that with a hangover!

Kate was great with the kids, a wonderful mum, but looking back now, I can see that it must have been hard for her as her hands were always full. I helped out where I could as one advantage of being a footballer is that you have a lot of free time, so I often picked the children up from school or nursery and we then had the afternoon free to do some fun family things, like going to the park or the zoo. We had lots of good days out and holidays over the years.

I have already mentioned that when I was growing up, times were hard, and I got what my parents could afford which wasn't a great deal. I'd get something on tick (a savings plan) from the catalogue which gave mum chance to save up. I was always grateful and appreciated how hard mum and nan worked, but as a kid it's difficult to understand why I wasn't able to have the same things that the other kids were getting. Now, I was in a privileged position where I could afford to buy things there and then, so the kids got spoilt and I enjoyed doing it. That look on their faces when I bought them something that they wanted was amazing – it was almost as good a feeling as scoring a goal. Almost, but not quite.

When they moved in with me, Jadine's dad used to pick her up every fortnight, but after six months, that stopped, and he didn't want anything else to do with her. I couldn't get my head around that. She was only six and it was really hard for her to understand, although she coped well. Roche's dad had died after being hit by a car when she was just months old, so I was the only father she had ever known. I treated them both like my own from day one and it wasn't long before they both started to call me dad because I was always there for them. They still call me dad today.

Kate and I had our first child together in June 1996, Jazzie, followed by Layla in June 2000, and in October 2004, we had a boy, Ziggy. I was there at the births of all my children. Jazzie and Layla were born in the summer, so that made things a bit easier. Good planning there! I

was supposed to beplaying for Leeds away at Brighton when Ziggy was born, but as soon as I got the call from Kate to say that she had gone into labour, I had a word with the gaffer and got on the train for the longest railway journey of my life. I made it just in time to see him born. Five kids and a beautiful partner – I'm a very lucky man!

CHAPTER 8
Nine inch nails

Introduction by Iwan Roberts. Former Leicester City Striker.

"I played alongside Julian for a couple of seasons and we formed a fantastic partnership. The City fans even created a chant about us:

> *Iwan is a Welshman, he wears a Welshman's hat,*
> *He lives next door to Joachim, in a council flat,*
> *He scores them with his left foot, he scores them with his right,*
> *And when he plays for Leicester, he scores all F***ing night!*

Now we didn't actually live next door to each other, but we did live on the same estate in Countesthorpe, Leicestershire – and we did score a LOT of goals.

Throughout my career, I always enjoyed playing with a small centre forward and Julian was an absolute joy to play with. Pace was his biggest asset – he was absolutely rapid – but he was also very good at reading the game, anticipating what was going to happen and his balance was ridiculous because of his low centre of gravity. I knew that his pace would create me goals and his movement would create me goals – he was the perfect strike partner for me.

He was very quiet on the pitch and hardly said boo to a goose, but don't be fooled by his size; he was as strong as an ox, with great upper body strength. Over the years I had to protect some of my strike partners and although I looked out for Jockey he didn't need any protection. For a start, defenders could rarely keep up with him! But if they did, he wouldn't take any shit and he had a streak in him that meant he could look after himself when he needed to.

He kept himself to himself in the dressing room and Steve Walsh used to give him some good natured banter – that's when you'd see Julian at his best, giving Walshy as good he got. I'd describe him as a silent assassin!

Off the pitch, Jockey is a lovely guy; quiet, unassuming and we looked upon him as a little brother. But he has to be the worst golfer that I have ever seen! I wouldn't say he was a keen golfer, but he played in the charity days and boys' days out and he was awful. He probably could have kicked the ball further than he was able to hit it with the club!"

*****

During the summer of 1994, there was again speculation linking me with various clubs who supposedly wanted to sign me. I don't know if the rumours were just paper talk or genuine interest, but it didn't matter to me. I was 100% focussed on keeping City up. I'd been there since I was a young kid and it was all I knew. All my friends were there, Leicester could offer me Premier League football and there was no reason to leave so I ignored the gossip.

Returning to Belvoir Drive for the start of pre-season, I was still euphoric following our promotion, yet doubts were creeping into my head and I began to wonder if we were actually good enough to stay up. We'd been schooled a couple of times against Premier League teams in the previous two seasons and we all knew that survival was going to be a tall order. We needed a few new faces and some additional quality, but we didn't have a great deal of money to spend and to be fair to Brian, he was loyal and wanted to give the lads who'd taken us up a chance.

The gaffer did make a couple of signings, spending a huge chunk of his transfer kitty on Notts County midfielder, Mark Draper. At £1.2 million Drapes became Leicester's record signing and a great one at that. We became firm friends and still are to this day. The only other summer signing of note was defender, Nicky Mohan, who joined from Middlesbrough for £300,000. It was always going to be tough to attract the players with the ability that we needed as we couldn't afford big transfer fees or wages and it didn't surprise us when the bookies made us favourites for the drop. Especially as four teams would be relegated in the 1994/95 season, rather than the usual three as the Premier League wanted to reduce the number of teams competing in it from 22 to 20. The previous play off winners, Swindon, had struggled and came straight back down and although we were a different team, it was a stark warning to us all of how tough it was going be.

Our biggest strength was the togetherness that we had as a team. We were all good mates who battled and fought for one another, but I worried that we'd need a bit more than that in the Premier League. That's not me putting down any of the lads, I was just being realistic.

Leicester City's first ever Premier League game took place at Filbert Street on 21st August 1994. Newcastle United were our opponents and the match was shown live on Sky Sports. I couldn't sleep the night before the game as I was too excited.

As soon as the match kicked off, my first thought was that Newcastle were incredible. The pace of the game was on a nother level and you could see the difference in quality, both individually and as a team. Andy Cole and Peter Beardsley were unbelievable up front for the visitors and they both scored in a 3-1 win for the North East side. The result was disappointing, but on a personal level I scored our goal which happened to be Leicester's first ever Premier League goal. At the time, I didn't really take in the significance of the goal, I was just pleased to score, and it gave me a little confidence boost that I belonged at the top level.

We lost our next two games, but worse than that, we lost our skipper, Steve Walsh, to another bad injury that meant he would miss most of the season. It was hard not to sympathise with Walshy. He had joined Leicester in 1986 when the club were in the old First Division. City were relegated at the end of the 1986/87 season and Walshy had fought for seven years to get back to the top-flight. He literally put his body on the line for us in the 1994 play off final and he had earned the chance to play in the Premier League. So we were all gutted for him on a personal level and devastated to lose one of our best players so early on in the season.

On 6th September 1994, I made my first start for England Under 21's in a home game against Portugal, up front with Robbie Fowler. While it was always special to represent my country, the fact that the match was held at Filbert Street made it even better for me as the ground was full of Leicester fans cheering me on. We drew 0-0 and all I can remember from the game is the disappointment that I hadn't scored.

Eleven days later, Leicester were sitting deep in the relegation zone, still without a win and with just one point from our opening five games. Not ideal when Ossie Ardiles' big-spending Tottenham Hotspur were coming to town. Spurs had a team full of big names, including Jurgen Klinsmann, Teddy Sheringham, Nicky Barmby and Sol Campbell in their line-up.

No one gave us a chance, but it was one of those games where everything just clicked and it's a match that City fans still look back on with fond memories. We beat Spurs 3-1 in a fantastic victory where I scored two goals. That result started a mini revival that took us out of the relegation zone for a short period of time and we began to wonder if maybe we could upset the odds and stay up.

Then Brian Little shocked us in November 1994, when he left to become the manager of Aston Villa, the club where he'd spent his entire playing career. I was gutted as he had given me my big break and was more like a father figure to me than a manager. He'd looked after me and had advised me off the pitch, even coming with me to help me choose my first car.

Things went from bad to worse, as I got injured while we were waiting for a new manager to be appointed.

We were in the gym at Belvoir Drive, had just finished a warm-up and began playing a five-a-side game. I had the ball and was twisting and turning when I dropped my shoulder to go the other way and I felt a little snap on the outside of my foot where my little toe was. It wasn't the pain that I noticed; it was the intense heat – my foot felt like it was burning up. I hobbled to the treatment room and they arranged for me to see a specialist who, after taking some X-rays, told me that I had pulled some tendons and advised me to rest for a couple of weeks before I could resume training.

I gradually started to walk and then jog, and I even made a few substitute appearances, but it felt worse than before. I went back to see the specialist who took some more X-rays before he again repeated that it was just damage to my tendons and that I needed to rest.

Meanwhile, the Board had acted swiftly and appointed Reading's Mark McGhee as our new manager. We got on well at the start. Not long after he joined, he called me into his office for a chat where he told me that I was a big part of his plans. That was music to my ears. Before Brian left, he had promised me a new contract, so I asked McGhee where I stood.

"You're injured now, but if you prove to me that you want to get fit and play football for me, I will honour your new contract," he told me. And he did. I signed a new deal before the end of the season.

On Boxing Day 1994, Liverpool rocked up at Filbert Street and I was devastated that I couldn't play against the team that I had supported as a kid. Before the match, I was sitting in the reception area of Filbert Street when the Liverpool squad arrived. Robbie Fowler, who I knew well from my England days, came over to say hello and ask about my injury. Robbie also introduced me to John Barnes, my boyhood hero. It was great to meet him, although I never got starstruck. I watched on from the stands as Robbie opened the scoring in a 2-1 defeat which was another nail in our coffin.

In January 1995, we had a home game against non-league Enfield in the third round of the FA Cup. I remained on the injury list and not in contention for the game, but I still had to report to the club, so I walked into the Fosse Restaurant to order some lunch before taking my seat in the stand, which was what you did if you weren't playing.

As I was waiting for my meal, I got a tap on the shoulder, turned around and saw Alan Smith, our physio, standing behind me.

"The gaffer wants you to be involved today," he told me.

I looked at him gone out and replied, "You know I'm not fit. I can barely walk!"

"I know, but McGhee wants you to have an injection to take the pain away so that you can play. Don't worry, he's not starting you. He just wants you on the bench."

It was 1.15 p.m. and kick off was at 3 p.m. I didn't have a choice, so I walked down to the treatment room where McGhee was standing alongside his coaching staff and the club doctor. They shut the door and McGhee explained that he wanted me to have an injection so he could put me on the bench because it would give the lads and the fans a big lift. I told him that I was struggling, still in pain and didn't want an injection, but I was a young lad and they put pressure on me. The doctor told me that it wouldn't do me any harm, so I reluctantly agreed.

McGhee and the coaches went back to the dressing room and the doctor started touching my foot and I was screaming in pain with the slightest bit of pressure. The doctor knew that I was genuinely injured, and he said, "I'm going to give you this injection, but even if your foot goes numb, I want you to say that it still hurts."

He injected me and my foot felt worse than before! The gaffer came in and asked how I was, so I told him.

"Thanks for trying," he said before walking back into the dressing room. I wasn't seen as a player or a person; I was used as a pawn really. McGhee wanted his best players in the team and that was all that mattered to him.

On the following Monday, the gaffer called me into his office and said that as the specialist couldn't find anything wrong with my foot, he was going to send me to see a different one. I think the implication was that I wasn't really injured which is ridiculous.

I can honestly say that I never, ever faked an injury in my career. I knew that footballers will have 10, maybe 15 years at best, and I wanted to play as many games as possible, often playing when perhaps I shouldn't have. I think most players can relate to this. You're always carrying a slight knock or feeling a little niggle. It's not very often that you feel physically great, but it was never enough to stop me playing. Unless I was properly injured that is.

So I went to the Nuffield Hospital in Leicester to meet a new specialist, Mr Chan. He took some X-rays and immediately found the problem.

"I'm not sure why this wasn't picked up before, but you've broken your foot, no wonder you've been in so much pain. You will need an urgent operation before it gets any worse," he told me.

I was in shock. Mr Chan told me that it could have been a whole lot worse for me if I'd played against Enfield - potentially ending my career!

A few days later I went under the knife and the operation went well. I had two long pins placed though my left foot and then it was put into a plaster cast. It was my first proper injury and I found it hard to deal with.

All sorts of things were going through my head; I started to worry if I'd ever recover and get back to my best. I had pace to burn and relied heavily on my speed and I wondered if that would be affected. Up until that point, everything had gone so well for me and then it all came to an abrupt halt and reality kicked in.

It is horrible being injured, there is nothing worse for a footballer. You're used to running around with the lads and being super fit, but when you're injured, you're isolated from the rest of the squad, you can't move and have to watch everyone else having a laugh and a giggle. There were half a dozen others injured, including Walshy, and we all supported each other. The results on the pitch weren't great and I felt so helpless seeing the lads struggle and knowing there was nothing I could do to.

After six to eight weeks of my leg being in plaster the pins were finally ready to come out. I reported to the hospital and sat on a bed while the surgeon sawed off the plaster cast. I looked down and saw two long nails through my foot, bent over the outside.

"We need to get these out today, so I'll be back in a few minutes," the surgeon said before walking out of the room.

"What happens now? Will I be put to sleep or will I be given a local anaesthetic?" I asked Alan Smith, who had gone with me.

"I'm not sure," he replied.

Five minutes later the surgeon walked back into the room, got a pair of pliers out of a draw, held them in one hand and grabbed my foot with the other. He then began to pull the nails out. The first one was really bent and it took three or four minutes of tugging before it finally came out. I was in agony! As soon as the nail was removed, blood started spurting out of the hole. It was like something out of a horror movie!

I had a right sweat on and asked for a break for a few minutes so that I could take a breather.

"No," was the immediate response from the surgeon. So I gritted my teeth and luckily the second nail came out in just 20 seconds which was a huge relief. I was even more relieved when he told me that I would make a full recovery.

When I began my rehab, my left leg was much smaller than my right and had lost all shape. It also felt very weak and I had to do lots of weights on my legs to build them back up before I could start training properly again. I still had a few weeks to go to get back to match fitness, but it was great to be back with the lads and able to run around and kick a football again.

Towards the end of the season, I lost a lot of respect for McGhee and our relationship started to deteriorate. One day, I received a call from the club receptionist asking me to report to the ground because the gaffer wanted to see me. I arrived at Filbert Street, knocked on the manager's door and walked in. Inside the office was McGhee, the chairman and the coaching staff. I thought, 'what's going on here?'

"We've had a phone call from a very good source who said that you've taken some sort of drug," McGhee said. I was too shocked to answer. I've never taken a drug in my life.

"Will you take a drug test?" McGhee asked.

"Of course," I replied.

"That's good because we've booked you in for one at 6 p.m. tonight," he said.

I was fuming. I knew that I didn't have anything to worry about with the test, but I was disappointed with the way it was being handled. He could have asked me one on one, he didn't need to bring everyone else into the room and I was frustrated that my word wasn't good enough. I had nothing to hide, so I went to the doctor's house in Kirby Muxloe that evening and took the test.

Two weeks later, the results came back and I got the all clear as expected. All I got from McGhee was, "Thanks for taking the test." There was no sorry for him not believing me or for embarrassing me like that. There were random tests at the training ground and after games, so it wasn't like I hadn't been tested before. I lost trust in the gaffer from that moment on.

McGhee brought some new players in, good players too, like Jamie Lawrence, Garry Parker and Mark Robins, and the lads kept battling away, but we lacked that little bit of quality and consistency that we needed if we wanted to survive.

I made my long-awaited comeback in the penultimate game of the season, but by that stage we had already been relegated. It had been a huge achievement to get to the big league, but we just couldn't get enough points on the board to stay up. Whilst it was disappointing, I knew that we had enough quality to get straight back up the following season.

CHAPTER 9
The end of an era

Introduction by Stefan Oakes. Former Leicester City Midfielder.

"*Julian is four years older than me, and when he was tearing it up in the first team, I was a schoolboy, dreaming of becoming a pro, like my older brother, Scott, who had made his Leicester debut in 1989.*

When I signed YTS forms, I was told that I was responsible for cleaning Steve Walsh and Jockey's boots – the captain and the star player - no pressure then!

Walshy was on at me all the time, "Yeah, Oakesy, they look good," but Jockey didn't really say much. Obviously, I made sure his boots were top notch all the time, so he never had any complaints although I'm not sure he'd have said anything even if they weren't! He was very shy, quiet and unassuming, still is really, but once he was on that football pitch, he was a real problem for the opposition with his rapid pace, and he was one of the most exciting players in Leicester's team.

Walshy used to give me his boots at the end of the season. Jockey's were the wrong size, but he made up for that with his generous Christmas tips. And when I say tips, I don't mean horse racing tips – that was never for me.

Jockey is a good lad and we've since crossed paths, playing alongside each other in legends' games where he is still one of the quickest players on the pitch, very sharp and you can tell he looks after himself. He hasn't changed a bit, is still very quiet and it takes a while for him to come out of his shell. He's definitely not a shouter, but when you get to know him he is a funny guy with a very dry sense of humour."

*****

The end of the season came at the wrong time for me as I was just getting back to full fitness and wanted, no, needed more games. So I was delighted when I found out that I'd been named in Ray Harford's England Under 21 squad for the Toulon Tournament which was to be held in France during June, 1995.

England had won the tournament in 1994 and we felt we had a good chance of retaining the trophy, especially with Harford naming a strong squad that included Phil Neville, Dean Richards and David Beckham.

We lost our opening group match 2-0 to Brazil, the eventual winners. Our second game of the tournament was a 2-1 victory over Malaysia in Six-Fours-les-Plages, a beautiful little island just off the Southern coast of France. It was a memorable occasion for me as I scored my first U21 goal, although I cannot recall anything about the actual goal! Chelsea's Andy Myers got the other one.

We beat Angola 1-0 two days later, thanks to a goal from Nicky Forster and that set up a semi-final tie against France, the hosts.

Olivier Dacourt and Robert Pires lined up for the French who proved too strong for us and they beat us 2-0. England finished third in the tournament and while we had obviously wanted to win it, I was pleased that I'd got some more competitive games under my belt as I battled back to full fitness.

When we returned for pre-season training in July, 1995, we knew that there would be some changes to the squad. Mark Draper had been outstanding for us and his form had earned him a call up to Terry Venable's England squad. With Euro 96 only a year away, we all knew that Drapes would be staying in the Premier League. Sure enough, Aston Villa came in for him and I was sad to see him go. I didn't know it at the time, but Villa had also made an approach for me which Leicester rejected immediately.

McGhee brought in Steve Corica and Scott Taylor, two quality midfielders, and we got off to a fantastic start to the new season. I scored my first goal of the season in a 1-0 win over Derby County that sent us to the top of the table.

I'm often asked to describe the feeling of scoring a goal – it's hard, but i'll try and try and explain it here.

I got so much of a high, it was like a drug. That feeling when the ball hit the back of the net was so addictive and I have found that it has been impossible to replace since I finished my playing career. Being a footballer is the best job in the world; you get a constant buzz, from the games, the fans, the grounds and goals and when you retire, that buzz goes and you can't get it back. Every now and then I'll see an old video of one of my goals and it brings the feeling back a little. Nothing in my life has ever come close to replicating that feeling of scoring a goal.

As a striker my aim was to score or assist a goal – that was always my primary focus when I stepped on to the pitch. You often hear footballers interviewed after a game when they have scored and they say something like, "Winning is the most important thing, it doesn't matter who scores the goals as long as we win." I can tell you now that, for me, scoring a goal was the most important thing. Nothing beat the feeling that I got when I heard the whooshing sound of the ball hitting the back of the net, followed a second or two later by the roar of the jubilant supporters.

If I scored and we won, well, it was the icing on the cake – there really was nothing better. It would put me in a good mood, I'd be full of confidence and excited for the next game.

The day after a match when I had done well was amazing. I enjoyed reading the daily papers to see what people were saying about me. It was a bit of an ego trip, seeing the nice things people were writing and I got a confidence boost seeing a good rating next to my name. It didn't matter if we'd won or lost though, I always read the papers. It was hard to digest when I'd had a bad game, but I always knew if I'd played well or not and had to be honest with myself and I used the feedback to improve.

At the end of September, we played Norwich City away and a young striker named Emile Heskey first experienced the euphoria of scoring a goal at senior level when he bagged the only goal of the game. Like me, Emile had made the progression from the Leicester City School of Excellence to the first team. He was a few years younger than me, but you could tell at that age that he was going to be a big star. I'd occasionally watch the youth or reserve games and he was head and shoulders above everyone else, literally with his strong build and his ability. It was nice to see another young lad breaking into the first team, although his arrival probably had a big factor in my later departure from Filbert Street.

During my time at Filbert Street, the club was particularly good at giving young players a chance: Scott Oakes, Carl Muggleton, Richard Smith, Neil Lewis, Russell Hoult, Sam McMahon and Emile, were just some of the former youth team players I played with who graduated from the youth team to the seniors.

Another promising young player who broke through was Stefan Oakes – brother of Scott, who had played for City when I was in the youth team – a classy midfielder with a sweet left foot. Although he didn't make his first team debut until 1998, I knew all about him because he was responsible for cleaning my boots. He did a good job and I'd like to think that I was a more generous tipper than the gaffer and coaches were to me!

I made my final England Under 21 appearance on 10th October, 1995 against Norway in the Viking Stadium, Stavanger. Andy Booth, Neil Shipperley and I led the line for the Three Lions in a 2-2 draw, with a young Ole-Gunnar Solskjaer finding the net for Norway. In total I made nine appearances for the Under 21s, scoring once.

No one told me that it was my final game, but I had turned 21 and I knew that Dave Sexton, the manager, wanted to give opportunities to the next generation of young lions, like Emile Heskey. I represented my country at Under 18, Under 20 and Under 21 level which I'm immensely proud of.

By November, Leicester had slipped to second in the table and I suddenly found myself in and out of the team. I was still young and the lads were playing well, so I didn't go banging on the manager's door to demand to play. Instead, I got my head down and worked harder to try and impress him. I don't know how I went from being one of the star players to a squad member. McGhee never explained why he wasn't picking me and I think it's fair to say that our relationship was frosty by then. Maybe my face just didn't fit which happens quite often in football. I don't know how he felt, but we certainly had our differences and I started to think that maybe it was time for me to leave.

But then just before Christmas, McGhee shocked everyone when he walked out on Leicester to join Wolves, even though we were challenging for promotion and Wolves were battling relegation. The fans were understandably angry and upset, but I was pretty happy and, if I'm being totally honest, I wasn't the only player who felt that way. It was time for a fresh start and a clean slate for everyone, especially those like me who weren't playing regularly.

There were a few rumours doing the rounds as to who the new gaffer would be before we were told that the former Norwich and Everton manager, Mike Walker, was coming in. He was introduced to the supporters' club and then at the last minute, the board changed their mind and appointed Martin O'Neill instead!

Martin injected some positivity back into the football club and I got on well with him. If you played well, he'd tell you and he was great at giving encouragement and turned out to be a fantastic appointment for Leicester. Unfortunately, I didn't get to work with him for very long.

Towards the end of February, 1996, I had a day off so I travelled back to Boston to spend some time with my mum. I arrived back at my home in Markfield, Leicestershire, around 6 p.m. and the minute I walked through the door I could hear the phone ringing. It was the gaffer.

"I've been trying to get hold of you all day," he began and I wondered what was going on. "I've had Brian Little on the phone. He's made an offer for you and while I don't want to sell you, I need some money to strengthen the squad and we don't have any. I've accepted the offer, but I won't force you to move if you'd prefer to stay. I will say this, though, you belong in the Premier League, you have worked with Brian before and I think it's the best move for you at this moment in time."

'Wow', I thought. I wasn't expecting that. I didn't really want to leave either. I knew that under O'Neill, Leicester were on the cusp of something great, but I agreed to go and speak to Brian. He told me that he'd come in for me half a dozen times over the past twelve months and he really wanted me to join him at Villa. I spoke to Drapes and he told me that Villa were a great club with a good team spirit so I decided to leave.

On 23rd February, 1996, I arrived at Belvoir Drive for the final time to collect my belongings and to say goodbye to the lads. It was really emotional and I had a very heavy heart. I'd been at Leicester since I was boy and in many ways I had grown up there, but on the flip side, I was excited to be going back to the Premier League and joining a massive club.

CHAPTER 10
Jockey Fart Pants

Introduction by Ian Taylor. Former Aston Villa Midfielder.

"Julian was the quickest thing I've ever seen! Everyone knew that speed was his biggest asset and that made him a handful for any defender, but what a lot of people didn't realise was how strong he was. We used to laugh and joke about his strength.

For me, as a midfielder, Jockey was a dream to play with. I knew that I just had to knock the ball down the sides and more often than not, he'd beat the defenders and get on the end of my pass. He was a massive asset for us.

He was often used as a substitute for Villa, but he eventually had a really strong period when he became a first team regular and scored a lot of important goals for us. There was one match against Coventry where he'd gone through, went round the keeper and was virtually on the by-line before somehow managing to screw it into the goal from a really tight angle. I remember watching on, just thinking, wow!

We were roommates for away trips which was nice as he was a genuinely good guy and never caused any trouble. Although, he'd never make the tea. Ever! That caused a few arguments and I also remember that he liked his sleep.

Jockey was one of those people who just got on with it, he never got too high or too low about anything. In the overall scheme of the dressing room, he was quite quiet, but there was a group of us, Tommy Johnson, Mark Draper, Jockey and myself, who went out together. He was the life and soul of that group and we always had a laugh."

I found it tough to join a new club because I'd been at Leicester for so long, it was all that I had ever known. My first day of training at Bodymoor Heath, Villa's training ground, felt a bit like the first day at a new school and I was terrified if I'm honest.

I knew that I'd have to prove myself to the supporters and the players and I didn't really know what sort of welcome I'd receive from either.

Villa were a massive club who had won the European Cup just 14 years previous and expectations were understandably high. Some of the players had huge reputations and I was worried about how I'd fit in as I didn't know anyone other than Mark Draper. I was very shy and kept myself to myself and meeting new people has never been easy for me. Yes, I knew the manager and coaching staff, but it's the players that you need to bond with because you're with them all the time.

Drapes was a great mate of mine and he introduced me to my new teammates before my first training session. They were a great set of lads and immediately made me feel part of the group. Luckily, there were no initiations for me to go through like there are at some clubs!

Football clubs often hold press conferences to introduce new signings – something else that I hated – but Villa didn't do one for me. I only had to do a couple of interviews for the local radio stations and newspapers which suited me fine.

The only nerves that I had were about meeting new people and speaking to the press; I didn't have any worries about my ability on the pitch and I couldn't wait to show the Villa fans what I could do.

The first thing that struck me about Aston Villa was the confidence running through the club. We were fourth in the Premier League at the time and still competing in both the FA and League Cups. Travelling to games, the lads would laugh and joke and make predictions about how many goals we would win by. It was a world apart from the last time that I'd been in the Premier League with Leicester, when we'd only won six games all season. The Villa lads expected to win every game. I had never experienced anything like that before and their confidence rubbed off onto me. Manchester United, Liverpool, Arsenal – it didn't matter who we were playing, we always felt that we could win.

The reason for their confidence was the sheer amount of quality that we possessed throughout the squad. When I looked around the dressing room, I could see that we had a different class of player to what I'd been used to. I don't mean any disrespect to my former teammates; it's just that we had a number of world class players such as Dwight Yorke, Mark Bosnich and Paul McGrath, and although we had some great players at Leicester, none of them were really world class.

Bosnich was a great goalkeeper who at times was impossible to beat outside the 18-yard box. We used to have a laugh with him during shooting drills at training. There was an unwritten rule that if your ball went wide you had to fetch it yourself as punishment for missing. As we ran past his goal, Bozzy would shout insults at us to try and wind us up. In return, I would try and lob him which was the ultimate embarrassment for any goalkeeper. If he caught the ball, he'd have someone boot it as hard as they could, as far away as possible and you'd have to go and get it whilst getting abuse from your teammates. That was payback for trying to take the piss. If you scored, though, it was a different story. Everyone would laugh at the keeper. Bosnich was good, but I still managed to lob him a few times.

Bozzy was as loud as you can imagine him being. He also gave me a new nickname within days of joining Villa. At Leicester, I was known as Jockey due to my small stature and my racehorse-like pace. I was also renowned for farting a lot and that's probably what most of my teammates remember most about me these days! One day, Bozzy called me 'Jockey Fart Pants' and the name stuck! It got to the stage where the lads would fart on the team coach knowing that I'd get the blame, even though it wasn't me.

A goalkeeper is only as good as his defenders and ours were exceptional, especially Gareth Southgate and Paul McGrath.

Southgate, who later became our captain, had joined Villa six months earlier as a central midfielder before Brian converted him in to a centre-back. A lot of captains go on to become managers or coaches and you could see that Gareth had that potential in him, so I am not surprised to see how well he has done as the

England manager. He was very intelligent, on and off the pitch, and everyone respected him. He was comfortable on the ball too but wouldn't hesitate to go in hard and win crunching tackles. Although Gareth comes across as very quiet and thoughtful in public, he was good at getting us all fired up before a game, a great leader.

Alongside Gareth in the centre of our defence was Paul McGrath. He was very quiet in and around the training ground, but he was so well respected and had such an aura around him. He made 40 appearances for us in the 1995/96 season and was also still playing for the Republic of Ireland which was incredible considering that his knees were gone which meant that he needed injections before every game and he couldn't even train with the lads. Instead, he'd come to the training ground and pedal away on the exercise bike on his own for an hour. That was it. But come match day he was as good as anyone. He made up for his lack of pace by the way that he read the game and his experience was vital for us.

Paul was a lovely guy too, you couldn't wish to meet a nicer person. I always remember he turned up at training the day after Jazzy was born with a little designer baby suit for her. What a lovely gesture.

Another senior pro was Andy Townsend. He was the captain when I first joined and a true leader. He was solid in the middle of the park, rallied the lads and led by example. With so many flair players in the side, we needed someone like Andy to battle away.

Ian Taylor was my roommate at Villa, a good lad and a great player. He was a box-to-box midfielder who scored some really important goals for us. Tayls had a good engine and was one of the most underrated players in the Premier League. Not many fans from other teams gave him the credit that he deserved, but he was without doubt one of our most important players and very popular with our supporters. I think he'd have done a good job for England, to be honest, and I'm not sure why he never got a call up.

The main man in the team was Dwight Yorke. He made headlines on the front and back pages and loved the attention. He was a very, very talented player who was on the top of his game and scoring lots of goals when I signed. I was only 21 and still learning my trade, so I looked up to Dwight. If I was on the bench or in the stands, I'd watch his movement and try and pick things up from him. We formed a good partnership up front.

Yorkey oozed confidence. He'd do things like stand in a bin in the dressing room and say, "I bet you £50 that I can do 100 keep ups with my shoulder and head without stepping out of this bin." Now, I liked a bet as much as the next man, but I was a bit too wise to fall for that. Someone else took on the wager and Dwight amazed us all by doing more than 100 keeps - incredible.

The training sessions were focussed, sharp and fast-paced, and I couldn't wait to start what I hoped would be a long and successful Villa career. I made my first appearance wearing the famous claret and blue shirt in a 3-3 draw away at Wimbledon on 24th February 1996, coming off the bench to play the final five minutes.

Four days later, I made my home debut against the defending champions Blackburn Rovers. I received a fantastic reception from the Villa faithful and the game couldn't have gone much better from my perspective. In the 55th minute, Drapes played a great ball out wide to Gary Charles who controlled it with his chest before whipping a cross into the Blackburn penalty area. I was unmarked and headed the ball into the back of the net from six yards. My teammates came over to congratulate me and it was a huge relief for me to get off the mark so early on in my Villa career. Gareth Southgate netted our second to give us a 2-0 win. A goal and a win against the champions – you won't be surprised to read that I snapped up every paper that I could get my hands on the following day!

The following week we played Liverpool at Anfield and I was named as a substitute. It was a big game as they were third and we were fourth, just three points behind them. We got off to the worst possible start and were 3-0 down inside eight minutes. We were chasing the game, so the gaffer brought me off the bench in the first half and put me up front alongside Dwight Yorke and Savo Milosevic. Unfortunately, we couldn't get back into the game and we lost a crucial match in our bid for European qualification. The only positive for me was that I got to play against my boyhood hero, John Barnes.

We didn't have time to dwell on that defeat as on 24th March 1996, we travelled down to Wembley for the League Cup Final. I had already played in the competition for Leicester which meant

73

that I was cup tied and unable to take part in the final. There were a few of us who weren't involved for various reasons, but the gaffer was great to us, making us all feel welcome and part of the occasion.

It was a great day out. I watched from the stands as we beat Leeds 3-0 with goals from Milosevic, Taylor and Yorke. I was as delighted as anyone to see us win a major honour and it reaffirmed my belief that I had joined a big club who were going places. I celebrated with the lads on the pitch after the game and we had a party afterwards to celebrate the victory.

Liverpool ended our dreams of a second final when they knocked us out of the FA Cup semi-final, but we maintained our strong league form to finish fourth in the Premier League, meaning that we had qualified for the UEFA Cup.

With the season over, I went away with Kate and the kids to Disneyland Paris. It was nice to treat them and see their excited faces on the rides and when they met their favourite characters.

During the season, football came first and I had to fit in my family around our fixtures. With the kids in either nursery or school during the week and me away playing games at the weekends, the summer break was the only real chance that I had to spend quality time with my family. It still wasn't easy as when the season finished the kids were still at school, so we probably only had about three weeks when we were all off at the same time. We always made sure that we got our holidays in sharpish.

I liked to enjoy myself during the summer months because the seasons were long and tiring and I looked forward to taking some time off to rest and recover. I'd usually take the first two weeks off where I'd do absolutely nothing. Then I'd start jogging again so that I wouldn't lose too much fitness or put on too much weight!

I always enjoyed fitness work and training, I still do. It's a good job really as I had to train every single day. The only thing that I didn't find fun was pre-season training because it was always punishing. Those first few sessions when we returned were gruelling; long distance running, hill running and a bit more running thrown in too. Did it get us fit? Yes. Was it enjoyable? Not at all!

I found the first three or four pre-seasons as a pro the hardest because I had to get to the required fitness level. I'd never been professionally fit, so I was starting from scratch. As I got more experienced it was a case of regaining my fitness which was a bit easier.

Euro 96 was the main talking point amongst the lads when we met up at the start of pre-season training. England had played brilliantly and almost reached the final before they lost to Germany in a cruel penalty shootout. Gareth missed the crucial penalty and when he returned to training, we made it clear to him that he had our support. It took a lot of bottle for him to take that penalty, not a lot of players would have fancied it in such a big game. Ok, so it didn't work out for him on the night, but it did make him stronger as a person and he quickly moved on and became an even better player.

Although, I'm not sure what he was thinking when he agreed to star in a TV advert for Pizza Hut! He was joined by Stuart Pearce and Chris Waddle, who had both missed spot kicks during the 1990 World Cup semi-final, as they were taking the piss out of themselves. I hope Pizza Hut paid him well because he took a lot of stick from the lads in the dressing room for that advert!

We already had a good team, so there were only a couple of new faces brought in to bolster the squad for the 1996/97 season: Fernando Nelson (right back) and Sasa Curcic (midfield).

We started the season well, but I found myself in and out of the side and didn't have the chance to stamp my authority on the team and show everyone that I could do. Although I scored in our third match of the season, at home to Derby County, a team that I always seemed to do well against, I found myself out of the team for the next game. The biggest frustration for me was that even when I had played well, I would get dropped for the following game because our Serbian striker Savo Milosevic had to play a certain percentage of matches to meet his work permit requirements. To be fair to the gaffer, he did pull me aside and tell me that it was out of his hands, and that I just needed to keep doing what I was doing and my chance would come. I trusted the gaffer and never went knocking on his door demanding to play. I was still young at the time, so I remained patient and kept working on my game.

On 23rd October 1996, we travelled to Highfield Road for a league game against Coventry. I opened the scoring with one of the best – and most bizarre – goals of my career. To this day, I still can't work out how I did it!

I was standing in the Coventry area on the left hand side when Alan Wright played a long ball into the box. I chased the bouncing ball, beating the defender, Paul Williams, for pace before Steve Ogrizovic, Coventry's keeper, came out. I sort of knocked it past him and the ball almost went out for a goal kick. I was falling backwards but managed to get enough of an angle to wrap my foot around the ball and kicked it towards the goal. I remember there was a photographer, sitting on his stool and I tumbled into him and almost knocked him over! The ball skimmed the post and crossed the line, despite the best efforts of a Coventry defender who was unable to clear it.

I'd actually forgotten about the goal until I saw it on social media recently and when I watched it, I thought, 'how on earth did I do that?' I could probably have tried that 100 times and not score it again.

Our league form throughout the season was generally good and while we weren't close to challenging for the title, we were always in and around the top six or seven positions. But, in contrast to the previos season, our performances in the cup competitions was extremely disappointing. We went out of the UEFA Cup in the first round, losing on away goals to the Swedish side, Helsingborg, and we also went out of both the League and FA Cups in the fourth round, to Wimbledon and to Derby.

Before transfer deadline day in 1997, Brian called me into his office and told me that he'd received an enquiry from Leicester City about my availability. The gaffer explained that he'd told Martin O'Neill that I wasn't available. I didn't want to leave Villa Park and Brian didn't want to sell me, so that was the end of the matter. However, if the gaffer had accepted an offer, it would have been very hard for me to turn it down and I would have more than likely gone back to Leicester.

I did go back to Filbert Street on 5th March 1997, but I was playing for the Villa against my former club. It was nice to return to where it had all begun for me, although it was strange walking into the away dressing room, instead of the home one, and lining up against people that I had known for years.

I was there to do a job for Villa and as soon as I took to the field all the emotion went out of the window. Brian had a tough time from the fans who still hadn't forgiven him for leaving back in 1994. My reception was more positive than anything else, though. I got the odd 'Judas', but in the main the fans were great to me and welcomed me back. I think that was because I had come through the youth ranks and they knew that I had always given 100% for them.

During the game there was a bit of banter between me and Walshy where I was telling him that he couldn't catch me! After the game we shook hands and I met up with my former teammates for a pint in the players' lounge. We lost that match 1-0 and we always seemed to struggle against Leicester. They became a bit of a bogey side for Villa.

I never really worried about who were playing against, teams or individual players. I was the striker so my mentality was to let them worry about me. Defenders often tried to use their size and intimidate me, but it never worked. My old youth coach, Steve Hunt, used to tell me not to show my opponents that they'd hurt me. So, when I got hit – which was often – I just got straight back up and smiled at the culprit. I knew that if I showed fear, they would go for me again.

No matter who we were facing, I always prepared in my usual way. The night before a game was intense. I would be thinking about the game all evening, so much so that I couldn't relax and I was probably burning up too much energy. On matchday mornings, I'd have breakfast around 9 am; cereal, toast, jam and honey – lots of carbs – and then I wouldn't eat again until after the game because I always liked to feel empty when I played.

In the dressing room before a match, someone would bring in a CD or cassette and I'd listen to that on my walkman. I was into reggae music, Marvin Gaye, Gregory Isaacs and of course, the legendary Bob Marley.

However, I remember bringing a Bob Marley CD into the dressing room once and putting it on the CD player, but it only lasted half a song before someone else switched it off because the lads wanted something a bit more upbeat to fire us up for the match.

Some players are superstitious with little pre-match rituals that had to be followed, others need to listen to loud music with a high tempo, while beating their chests and shouting, in order to pump themselves up for a game. I was different; I had no superstitions and preferred to be nice and relaxed before a game, so I'd just find a quiet part of the dressing room where I'd sit and think about the task ahead.

I always got a few nerves before a match, I think most players do. I was never worried about who I was coming up against, my nerves were because I wanted to play well. Football is strange in that you can train and prepare and do everything right all week, but you never know how you're going to perform until you cross that white line.

The games themselves usually went by in a bit of a blur. Supporters often appreciate the physical exertions we players go through, but football is mentally exhausting too. The concentration levels are intense, especially at the highest level when there is so much at stake. One lapse in concentration could lead to a very costly mistake, so you have to be switched on all the time. Often after a game, I could only remember parts of what I'd done.

I was never affected by the large crowds that I played in front of. Most of the time, you don't hear the specifics of what people are singing and shouting, unless the ball is out of play or you're on the bench, so when you're playing you just hear noise. I remember the first time that I heard my name chanted – "Julian, Julian" – while I was playing for Leicester which gave me a real boost. That chant followed me around clubs. The City fans also came up with a funny song about me living next door to Iwan Roberts (my strike partner) in a council flat. I also experienced a few boos from time to time, but I always managed to block them out, so it didn't put me off my game.

After a match I would usually go into the players' lounge to meet up with any friends and family who had come to watch me play; only for half an hour or so to show my face and then I'd drive back home and spend the rest of the evening with my family. If I'd scored I'd watch *Match of the Day,* but I didn't watch it all the time, just now and then to see how the other teams were doing. I've never really been a good watcher of football and I rarely sit down to watch a full game on the TV.

I don't play computer games either, like a lot of players do. I've never really seen the appeal, although my son, Ziggy, has often tried to get me involved. Probably because I'd be easy to beat! I used to find it funny when people stopped me in the streets to tell me that I was good value on Championship Manager or FIFA!

To unwind, I enjoyed a flutter (we'll get to that in more detail later) and I loved to play snooker. Ronnie O'Sullivan was my favourite player; he had an edge to his game, with his fast and attacking style of play and I'd travel to the Crucible to watch him compete (and likely win) in the World Championships. A lad that I knew from Boston, Del Boy, was Ronnie's coach and I found out through him that Ronnie wanted to meet me.

I met up with Ronnie one night in London after a group of friends and I had been to Royal Ascot. He was out with a few others, including Phil Tufnell, the cricketer, and we went to a few bars together. Ronnie and I hit it off, had a good night and since then, if I'm ever attending one of his matches, he'll come over and have a chat with me which is nice.

I scored my obligatory goal against Derby in a 2-1 defeat on 12th April 1997. It was my third and final goal of the season.

We finished the 1996/97 campaign in fifth place and again qualified for the UEFA Cup. I was frustrated that I only played 15 times because I knew that I would be able to make more of an impact if I played more regularly. With one of our strikers, Tommy Johnson, leaving to join Celtic, I felt confident that I'd have a decent run of games during the following season.

And then we signed Stan Collymore for a club record £7million!

CHAPTER 11
Villain of the year

Introduction by Brian Little. Former Aston Villa Manager.

"I remember the first time I realised how quick Julian was. We did a little session in training, and I joined in the running. I was right at the back, so I thought I would have some fun with the lads. I shouted, 'Everyone turn around and race to the goal. If anyone finishes behind me, you'll be fined.'

Now, I had a twenty-five-yard head start in a seventy-five-yard race, but within seconds, I saw this flash as Julian ran past me. I could not believe it. What was incredible is that he was just as fast with the ball."

*****

Stan Collymore was a phenomenal player, an England international and at one time, holder of the British transfer record. We all knew that he had the ability, but his off-field problems often made bigger headlines. That was Stan – it came with the territory. He was a good lad in the dressing room and I got on well with him, even though it put me in a very difficult position.

I wanted Aston Villa's team to be as strong as possible because I wanted us to do well in the league and win trophies, but it was hard when good players came in to play in my position. I'd be lying if I said that I wasn't worried about my future at the club with Stan and Dwight – both fantastic strikers – ahead of me. On paper, I was a big outsider to play and no one outside the club gave me the time of day. I saw it as a challenge, a big test and an opportunity for me to learn from two top quality players. I remained confident in my ability and I think it spurred me on. I always wanted to be out there on the pitch, but if I wasn't, I'd be there cheering the lads on, itching to get back onto the pitch. I made a promise to myself that I would seize the opportunity once it came my way.

Stan wasn't the only new face coming in that summer as my former teammate Simon 'Larry' Grayson joined us from Leicester. With Brian Little, Allan Evans, me, Drapes and now Larry it was becoming a bit like a Leicester old boys' club! Larry had continued to improve at Leicester and had captained the side when they won the 1997 League Cup Final, so I knew that we were getting a quality player. He still lived in Leicester, like me, so we car shared into training and to matches together.

Despite the pre-season optimism, we got off to a dreadful start, losing our first four matches. We finally got our first win of the season on 30th August 1997 against Leeds and followed that up with victories over Barnsley and Derby – my first goal of the season was the winner against the Rams, again.

With three wins on the bounce, we expected to kick on but our season never really got going. We'd beat Bolton and then lose to Wimbledon, beat Everton before losing to West Ham. I can't put my finger on why we were so inconsistent. The only positive for me was that I was getting more game time. On 6th December 1997, I had already matched my previous season's tally of three when I scored our final goal in a 3-0 win at home to Coventry. I enjoyed playing alongside both Dwight and Collymore. They were both great players who would take defenders out of the game which created a lot of space for me to exploit.

Three days after the Coventry game, we beat Steaua Bucharest 2-0 at home to knock them out of the UEFA Cup. We'd already seen off Bordeaux and Athletic Bilbao, so we were through to the quarter final. The UEFA Cup was a nice distraction from our stuttering league form.

By February 1998, we had fallen to 15th in the league, with some pundits suggesting that we were in danger of getting drawn into a relegation battle. We knew that we had more than enough ability within the team to play ourselves out of trouble and the supporters were great, continuing to back us as they always did.

It helped that we had an exciting team who played some great football and we all knew that we were only a couple of wins away from turning things around.

But then on 24th February 1998, Brian Little dropped a huge bombshell when he announced that he was resigning as Villa manager with immediate effect. I don't know all the ins and outs, I just think that he had had enough. To say that I was shocked is a huge understatement. I had finally got back into the team, was playing well and now I was going to have to try and impress another new manager.

When Brian left Leicester, Mark McGhee had come in and it didn't really work out for me, so I didn't know what to expect this time around. Mentally it was hard; I waited to hear the name of the new gaffer and wondered if my face would fit. Will I know him? Will he rate me? A new manager might result in a change of clubs for me, which could mean moving house, new schools for the kids, starting all over again. I was settled at the Villa, loved the club and didn't want to leave.

Ruud Gullit, who had just been controversially sacked as Chelsea manager, was one of the high-profile names linked with the vacancy, but it was a familiar face who actually got the job, just one day after Brian left – John Gregory.

After following Brian to Villa to be a coach, Gregory had gone to Wycombe to cut his managerial teeth and been a success. I was delighted that he was coming in as I knew him very well and knew that he rated me. How many players can say they've cleaned their managers' boots? It was the perfect appointment for me, and a great fit for Villa, someone who knew the club inside out having played for us and been a coach. If Doug Ellis, our chairman, had asked me who I wanted to be our new manager, I'd have probably said Gregory, so I couldn't have been happier.

On his first day, he introduced himself to the lads before training and then he arranged individual meetings with us so that we knew where we each stood. When it was my turn, I went into his office, shook his hand and took a seat. He told me that he knew my contract was up at the end of the season, but he didn't have any intention of letting me go anywhere. I was in his plans and he told me that he'd sort out an extension for me in the near future. It was music to my ears and gave me a huge boost.

Gregory's first game in charge was at home to Liverpool who were sitting in fourth place. When he announced the team, most of us were surprised as he went with a very attacking line up with three strikers: Dwight, Stan and me.

Despite conceding early doors through a Michael Owen penalty, we fought back to win 2-1. It was a fantastic team display and Collymore was Man of the Match, scoring both goals against his former club.

Our next game was the UEFA Cup quarter final first leg, away at Atletico Madrid, in front of 55,000 hostile supporters – a huge test. When we landed in the Spanish capital, Dwight got stopped at passport control and the customs officials wouldn't let him through, saying there was a problem with his Trinidad and Tobago passport. The rest of us were waiting at the baggage carousel wondering if we'd be playing a big match without one of our best players. Eventually, Doug Ellis got involved and Dwight was allowed through.

Yorke and Collymore started the game up front, with me on the bench. We were 1-0 down when I came on to replace Stan in the second half. Gregory's instruction to me was to run at their defence and that's exactly what I did. I had a good chance minutes after coming on, but I hit it straight at the keeper. It was my first touch of the ball and I was probably a bit rusty. It's hard coming on as a sub in a game like that which was very different to the Premier League. The tempo wasn't quite as quick as domestic football, but they kept the ball so well and made us chase after them. I did well though and caused them a lot of problems with my runs down the right-hand side. It was clear that they were scared to death of my pace, but we just couldn't manage to force an equaliser and lost 1-0.

After the game I was asked to swap shirts, although I can't remember who. It was the first time I'd ever exchanged shirts. I never asked anyone to swap with me, I was always a bit too embarrassed to be honest, but if someone asked me, I was always happy to.

I regained my place in the starting line-up for our next league match on 8th March 1998, away to Chelsea live on Sky Sports. In the second half, Mark Draper passed the ball to me just inside the Chelsea area. I had a bit of time to control it, shimmied and then hit it past Ed De Goey into the back of the net. It was the only goal of the game.

I started in our next two matches and Gregory kept me in the starting line-up for the return tie against Madrid. Spain international Jose Caminero gave the visitors the lead in the 28th minute. We fought back and Ian Taylor scored a deserved equaliser with twenty minutes left on the clock. Two minutes later, Collymore put us in front on the night, but it wasn't enough and Atletico eventually went through on away goals. We put everything into that game and didn't deserve to go out, but that's football. Sometimes you play well and don't win, other times you play poorly and win. We just had to forget it and move on. Although we knew the rules going into the match, the away goals rule is a harsh way to lose and I'm pleased to see that it has been scrapped for the 2021/22 season.

We managed to put that disappointment behind us and went on an incredible run in the league that saw us lose just once in our final eight games. I scored three goals during that run which improved my confidence. There was no secret to it really; the more I played, the more I scored. I couldn't develop if I wasn't playing regularly which is why I'm not a fan of squad rotation. With each game under my belt, I could feel my fitness and sharpness improve and it all started to come together for me.

We had another debutant before the season finished, a young defender named Gareth Barry. Gareth was pretty quiet and although he wasn't the quickest, he read the game so well, especially for a young lad. He had been training with the first team for the bulk of the season and he had stood out, so we knew that it wouldn't be long until he made his first team debut, which he did on 2nd May 1998 against Sheffield Wednesday, aged just 17. In those days he was used as a defender, but he could play anywhere really; left back, left wing, centre midfield – nothing fazed him. He had bags of confidence, a sweet left foot and I'm not surprised that he went on to have the career he did.

Our form in the second half of the season had shot us back up the table and we finished in a decent seventh position, qualifying for the UEFA Cup again. I scored eight goals in 28 appearances, my best return for Villa at that stage and so I went in to see Gregory to discuss the new contract that he had promised me.

My agent was on his honeymoon at the time and because I knew Gregory well, I agreed to go to a meeting without him. We negotiated, toing and froing, but the deal wasn't quite right for me. I wasn't being greedy, but I felt that I deserved a bit more than I was being offered. I had been playing well and was becoming a regular under Gregory, but the gaffer said that he wanted to dangle a carrot in front of me to keep me hungry. Everyone knew that Dwight and Stan were on big money, although I wasn't expecting to be on anywhere near their wages because they were higher profile and I didn't have their experience.

But, in my view, it's what you do on the pitch that matters and I'd scored the same number of goals as Stan, yet played fewer games, during the 1997/98 season. I wasn't asking for the world and eventually we came to an agreement.

I signed a new deal worth £7000 a week, a good wage, of course, but a fraction of what a lot of my teammates were earning – some were rumoured to be on £30,000. Gregory told me that if I had a good season during the 1998/99 campaign, he'd rip up the contract and give me a new and improved one. It was down to me to go out and earn myself a better deal. I agreed because I was confident in my ability and I'd known him since I was a teenager. I trusted him. Looking back now, I really wish that I hadn't.

Gregory brought in Alan Thompson, a left midfielder from Bolton in the summer of 1998. He was a good signing, but it was a departure that made the biggest headlines when Dwight Yorke left us to join Manchester United for £12,600,000 in August.

Dwight had been our top scorer for the previous three seasons and I knew that he'd be a huge loss. Even though it meant there would less competition for me – especially as Savo Milosevic also left – I'd have preferred him to have stayed. Still, I saw it as the opportunity that I had been looking for to cement myself in the first eleven, although I knew I'd have to fight for the spot because no one has the right to just turn up and expect to play.

We couldn't have got off to a better start to the 1998/99 campaign. I scored our first goal of the season in our second match, a 3-1 win against Middlesbrough and I scored again in our next game, a 1-0 victory away at Sheffield Wednesday. Things got even better when we moved to the top of the table on 12th September 1998 following a 2-0 win over Wimbledon.

Desite the good start, Gregory went back to the transfer market and brought in Paul Merson (attacker) and Steve Watson (defender) as reinforcements and both became big assets for us.

Our UEFA Cup campaign kicked off with a 6-2 aggregate win over Norwegian side, Stromsgodset, setting up a second round tie against Celta Vigo. I scored the first European goal of my career in a 1-0 home leg victory, although we lost 3-1 in the second leg to go out of the competition.

In November, we were still top of the league and still unbeaten when Gregory signed England international, Dion Dublin from Coventry City, to try and keep us there. Although Dion was able to play in defence, he joined me up front and we formed a great partnership, in fact, it was the best partnership in all of my time at the Villa.

He was a confident striker and he'd talk to me a lot and share his experience. It was the typical big man/little man strike force, like the ones that I had enjoyed with Steve Walsh and Iwan Roberts at Leicester. When the ball came to him in the air, 90% of the time he would win the header, so I knew where I had to be. He was good with his feet too and used his strength to hold the ball up for me. We worked on things in training, of course, but we just clicked naturally and developed a good understanding of one another.

There is always room for improvement and because I was a quick player, I had perhaps relied on my speed too much, rather than building up my football intelligence. Dion taught me more about the game and was a massive help. I was a similar player to Darren Huckerby, who he'd partnered at Coventry, so I was probably a good fit for Dion, too.

On 5th December 1998, Manchester United turned up at Villa Park for a top of the table clash. My former international teammate, Paul Scholes, opened the scoring, and I grabbed a deserved equaliser in the second half. The draw kept us at the top and we were still there on Christmas Day.

I was enjoying a good run in the side, was gaining more experience and I was in the form of my life. Form is so important. If you've gone half a dozen games without scoring, it hurts. You might be setting up others and playing well, but strikers are judged on goals. When you're out of form, your luck goes too.

You hit the post more often and the goalies pull off world class saves. When that happened, my answer was to work harder and to train more. That's what I had done previously; stayed behind after training for 15-20 minutes of finishing practice, running through different scenarios. I'd do that three times a week and I knew that I'd eventually get my rewards. The 1998/99 season was when all my hard work finally paid off.

After Christmas, our form declined and by the end of February our title challenge was over. It was difficult to challenge the teams like Chelsea and Manchester United who had the spending power to build an entire squad full of quality players. Our best starting eleven was as good as anyone's, but we just didn't have enough depth to deal with the inevitable injuries and loss of form that all clubs experience. We lacked the consistency that the top, top sides had and we didn't have enough players in the side who had experience of winning league titles and trophies.

Despite our poor form, Aston Villa made history on 27th February 1999 when we became the first Premier League team to field an all-English eleven. Even the three substitutes who came on were English.

Our line-up was: Michael Oakes, Steve Watson, Gareth Southgate, Riccardo Scimeca, Alan Wright, Paul Merson, Ian Taylor, Simon Grayson, Lee Hendrie, Dion Dublin and me. We lost 4-1 to Coventry, but the team selection received a lot of media coverage because it was so rare, even in those days. I can't see it ever happening again, most teams would probably struggle to pick six English players in their starting line up now!

It was during the 1998/99 season when I got involved in a Chinese restaurant in Leicester. I had become friendly with a Chinese bloke who had found a vacant restaurant on New Walk in the City Centre and he asked me if I wanted to invest with him. I thought 'why not?' It had been shut down for six months and the building was up for lease, so I bought in with him. We called it Happy Valleys. He ran the day-to-day operations and I put the money in. I'd go there three or four times a week to eat, show my face and talk to the customers. A Chinese restaurant and a Premier League footballer doesn't sound like the best combination, but luckily, I've always been able to eat anything I want and not put weight on.

A few things went wrong, though and my mate had to sell up, so I contacted my old teammate Steve Walsh, who bought his share. We'd formed a good strike partnership and thought we could become successful business partners too. We renamed the place Walshy's and things started off well; we were reasonably busy and making a couple of quid, but it didn't last long.

It was a lot of hard work and expensive to run so we brought in another investor, Shaun Taylor, who had landed a big windfall on the lottery. We couldn't turn it around though and in the end it was draining money and we had to pull out a few years later. Walshy and Shaun could walk away but the lease was in my name. I had signed up for a £45,000 a year lease that still had ten years to run. I couldn't afford to keep it going so I closed the restaurant down and then managed to convince the landlord to write off the lease. I handed the keys back and felt so relieved. Sadly, it wasn't the last bad investment I made.

On 6th April 1999, I scored at Filbert Street for the first time since leaving Leicester. Lee Hendrie had given us the lead and I got our second. It was a strange experience, running to the cheering away fans and hearing the jeers of the City fans sitting in the Kop. It's a controversial thing to do these days, celebrating when you score against your former club, but for me, if you score a goal, you deserve to celebrate it as long as you don't go overboard. I celebrated every single goal I scored, my job was to score goals - that was what I was paid to do - so why wouldn't I celebrate? It doesn't mean you should rub the supporters' noses in it, though and I think Emmanuel Adebayor probably went too far when he scored for Manchester City against his former club, Arsenal, and ran the entire length of the field just to wind up the Gunner's fans!

I scored five goals in our final seven matches which helped us to achieve a sixth-place finish. After our strong start, it was a big disappointment and it meant that we failed to qualify for Europe for the first time since I'd been at Villa.

On a personal level, I enjoyed the best season of my career, finishing as Villa's top scorer with 16 goals and I won the Player of the Year award too. People were saying nice things about me and I didn't want to go on holiday, I just wanted to carry on playing football and couldn't wait for the new season to begin.

By the time the 1999/00 season kicked off, we had a new number one.

Mark Bosnich left us to re-join Manchester United. Bozzy was a great keeper, a safe pair of hands, and he was going to be a huge loss. It was a good move for him because United had just won the treble and they needed a replacement for Peter Schmeichel. Although it was never going to be easy for him to replace someone like Schmeichel, a lot of folk expected him to kick on and establish himself as one of the best in the world. I'm not really sure why it didn't work out for him at Old Trafford.

A couple of weeks later, we signed our new goalkeeper, David James, for £1.8 million. Jamo was a more than adequate replacement, he was a regular in the England squad and was approaching his peak. Like Bozzy, you certainly couldn't accuse him of being shy! He was incredibly vocal – on and off the pitch – and commanded his area well. He was a great character and an asset to the dressing room, as well as out on the pitch and we gained a new member of the card school too! Jamo was his own man, did a bit of DJ'ing on the side and was a bit eccentric – like most keepers are! Apparently Jamo was the man responsible for those shocking cream Armani suits that Liverpool wore before the 1996 FA Cup final – I don't think I was alone in being grateful that we kept our familiar dark suits at Villa!

Our season got off to a great start with wins over Newcastle and Everton (I scored in both games) as we looked to improve on last season's sixth place finish.

At the end of September, we lost to Leicester (our bogey team) and that defeat started a nine-game run without a victory in the league.

Fortunately, our cup form was strong and on 13th October 1999, I scored our first goal in a 3-0 win against Manchester United in the third round of the League Cup. It was Mark Bosnich's first game back at Villa Park since leaving in the summer and he received a hostile reception from the fans which I felt was harsh as he'd been a great servant to the club.

I scored in the fourth round against Southampton and again in the quarter final as we beat West Ham 3-1.

We were drawn against Leicester City in the semi-final and although we were considered to be the favourites, we drew the home leg 0-0 and lost the return fixture 1-0. I always wanted to do well against Leicester and I was desperate to get back to Wembley, so it was bitterly disappointing to go out. But if anyone had to knock us out, I'm glad that it was City and I was as delighted as anyone when they went on to beat Tranmere and win the trophy.

We were also doing well in the FA Cup, beating Darlington, Southampton, Leeds, Everton and Bolton, to reach the final for the first time since 1957.

The cup runs gave us some confidence and our league form turned around. Despite our early season woes, we only lost twice in the final 21 league games and finished sixth.

I was playing well, scoring goals and enjoying my football. I won a few Man of the Match awards and with Euro 2000 on the horizon, I was asked a few times about my chances of a call up to the England squad. I gave the typical response that playing well for Villa was my priority - which it was - but inside I felt that I could offer something to my country. Although I was playing well, it wasn't good enough in the eyes of Kevin Keegan, so I never received a call up. To be fair, England were spoilt for choice up front – even Robbie Fowler struggled to get a game and he was scoring thirty goals a season!

I remember Merse gave an interview saying that he thought I had a good shout, but it wasn't meant to be. I couldn't have played much better and it dented my confidence a bit as I was desperate to play for England, having done so well at Under 18, Under 20 and Under 21 level. I didn't know what more I could do. I wasn't the only one though, Mark Draper and Ian Taylor were two others who should have received at least one cap. These days you see players receiving call ups after only making a handful of appearances. It was much harder back then.

Thinking that my international dreams were over, I received a phone call out of the blue from a representative of St Vincent and the Grenadines, who asked me if I would be interested in playing for them in their forthcoming World Cup Qualifiers. My dad had been born there, so I was eligible, and I thought, 'why not?' England would have been my first choice, obviously, but if i couldn't play for them, St Vincent was an opportunity for me to play international football. I didn't know it at the time, but that decision marked the beginning of the end for me at Villa Park.

**My goal against Portsmouth helped send
Leicester to Wembley in 1993.**

I always enjoyed playing (and scoring) against Derby County.

Unbelievably, I was sent off for this altercation with
Colin Caulderwood! My City room mate, Steve
Thompson, is charging in to help.

Premier League here we come. Getting my hands on the
play off trophy in 1994 was an amazing feeling.

England finished third in the 1993 World Youth Cup.

The 1993 England under 18 from left to right:
Back row: Kevin Gallen, Kevin Sharp, Chris Day, Andy Marshall,
Sol Campbell, Rob Bowman, Nicky Butt.
Front row: Me, Paul Scholes, Noel Whelan, Jamie Forrester, Chris Casper,
Darren Caskey, Robbie Fowler, Mark Tinkler and Gary Nevile.

Receiving a celebratory hug from David Beckham after scoring for England Under 21s in 1995.

Winning the 1993 Under 18 European Championship with England was a proud moment for me.

Scoring against Peter Schmeichel at Old Trafford is no mean feat.

There is no better feeling than scoring a goal.

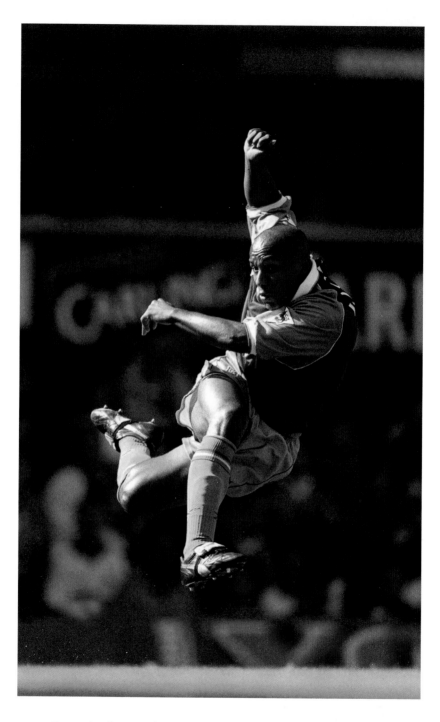

I practised my technique, but I blessed with natural ability.

I got my first taste of European football at Aston Villa. Here I am
playing against Atletico Madrid in 1998.

Every boy dreams of playing in an FA Cup final. I was devastated
that we lost 1-0 to Chelsea in 2000.

I enjoyed my best spell at Coventry during the 2003/04 season.
The fans were always great towards me.

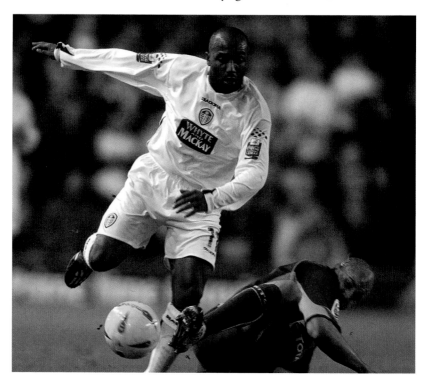

I didn't play as often as I would have liked during my time with Leeds.

I couldn't stop scoing during my loan
spell at Walsall.

I moved to Darlington just days after scoring twice against
them whilst playing for Boston United.

I played for final professional game for Darlington against
Rochdale on 17th May 2008.

I never expected to feature in a Hollywood movie, but here I am!

CHAPTER 12
International dreams and Hannibal Lector

Introduction by Dion Dublin. Former Aston Villa Striker.

"*I joined Aston Villa in 1998 and linked up with JJ. He worked very hard in training and was a joy to play with. JJ was a good reader of the game, ran very, very fast and could strike the ball harder than most people that I played with. I don't know what it was, but we just hit it off instantly and quickly formed a great partnership – I'd flick it on, he'd get on the end of it and score.*

There was a natural side to it, but under John Gregory we spent many hours on the training ground working on our movement and positioning, and we soon developed a good understanding of where each other would be. Our strengths complimented each other; I was a big communicator; JJ was a good listener and between us we scored a lot of goals.

Off the pitch, JJ is a normal down to each lad. We shared an affection for Leicester; I grew up in the city and Julian had learnt his trade at Filbert Street. We often went out together for a few beers, a meal or we'd just sit down and talk. A good bloke and very funny when you get to know him, although JJ did tell the occasional bad joke!"

*****

Once I'd agreed to represent them, St Vincent and the Grenadines contacted the English FA to request permission for me to play for them. The FA said that they had no objections, so I applied for a new passport and as soon as that came through in April 2000,

I received a call up for a World Cup Qualifier against St Kitts. I couldn't wait.

The only issue was that St Vincent's fixtures were not aligned to the international calendar, so my call up meant that I would miss an important league game against Tottenham Hotspur. The call up had come through to Villa, so the club were aware of it and they had never stopped anyone representing their country before, so I thought everything was ok.

My agent, Hayden Evans, and I travelled down to Heathrow and boarded the plane for the long flight to the Caribbean island. My nan and grandad still lived out there and I was looking forward to seeing them after the match.

We were halfway through the flight, I was relaxing, listening to some music when I heard a message over the plane's speakers asking me to make contact with a stewardess. When I did, I was told that an important phone call had come through for me from the St Vincent's FA and I needed to call them back urgently. I phoned them from the plane, and they said that FIFA had informed them that because I had played for England at Under 21 level, I wasn't eligible to represent them. I wasn't happy. I had been told that everything had been cleared, only for them to tell me mid-air that I couldn't play. It was a very cruel way of ending my international dreams. A few years later the rule changed, but it was too late for me by then. When we landed, I decided to stay for the week anyway, so that I could see my nan and grandad and meet some other relatives on my dad's side.

I'm still bitterly disappointed when I reflect on that incident. I recently heard that I am in the list of top ten Premier League goal scorers without a full international cap, along with Kevin Campbell and Paolo Di Canio. Not bad company to be keep though, I suppose.

When I arrived back in the UK, the newspapers were full of stories saying that Villa knew nothing about my call up until the day I flew out and that John Gregory wasn't happy with me. That wasn't true at all. I understand that Gregory would have preferred me not to travel half-way around the world, but sometimes you have to do things for yourself and that's what I did. He never had a problem with any of our other international players flying off to play for their country, so I don't know why he got the hump with me but he did.

Gregory's way of paying me back was sticking me on the bench for the FA Cup final against Chelsea and I was fuming. I had started in every round apart from the third and I'm convinced that he'd have picked me had I not missed the Spurs game. I knew I wasn't going to start every single game, but he didn't even explain to me why I had been dropped.

I was absolutely devastated because as a kid, the FA Cup was massive. Growing up, I'd look forward to Cup final day and would watch every single minute of the build-up; from the players boarding the coaches and driving up Wembley Way, to the singing of the National Anthem and Abide With Me. I remember dreaming that I would be involved one day and although I was there, Gregory's treatment of me took the shine off what had been a lifelong dream.

I didn't let my disappointment show, though, as I was still part of the squad and was 100% focussed on the game. There was a big media presence around the hotel that we were staying at in Oxhey, just outside Watford, and quite a few of the lads were giving interviews. You won't be surprised to read that I didn't do one!

Although I'd already played at Wembley four times, I was older, wiser and more experienced than I had been for the play off finals and I was determined to soak up the atmosphere and make the most of the occasion.

After breakfast on the morning of the match, we went for a walk in the grounds of the hotel and there was a good amount of laughing and joking from the senior pros like Paul Merson and Dion Dublin, which helped put some of the younger lads at ease. We were a confident group whoever we played and the atmosphere was quite relaxed.

For normal games, you go on to the pitch for a warm-up and to kick a ball about for a bit before the match. At the Cup final, we walked onto the pitch in our suits which is a bit strange as there isn't really anything to do other than have a look around. Some of the lads took the programme on to the pitch to read, but I've never really been a big reader, so I just looked around and tried to take everything in.

We then went back to the changing room to put our kit on and to listen to Gregory's final instructions and then it was time to walk on to the pitch. The tunnel at the old Wembley stadium was behind the goal at the end which the Villa fans occupied. The noise as we emerged was deafening, so much louder than the semi-final had been just a few weeks earlier.

It got even louder when the National Anthem was played as both sets of fans joined in. I was never very comfortable singing, but I didn't need to as I was standing next to Dion Dublin and he was belting it out! The hairs on the back of my neck were standing on end and I was raring to go, but instead of lining up on the centre circle for kick off, I had to make my way to the bench.

We were considered underdogs by most neutrals. Chelsea's star-studded line-up featured huge names such as the Ballon D'or winner, George Weah, and World Cup winners, Franck Leboeuf and Marcel Desailly, but we were also a good side, difficult to beat and worked well as a team, so we felt that we had a chance.

The first half was very tight and we went in 0-0 at half time. Chelsea started to edge it after the break, taking the lead early in the second half but the goal was disallowed, fortunately for us. With just 15 minutes left on the clock, Roberto Di Matteo did put Chelsea in front. Benito Carbone had a chance to equalise soon after, but his shot was cleared off the line.

With ten minutes to go, Gregory brought me on for Carbone. It was good to get on, but I didn't really have time to make a difference as we were chasing the game and Chelsea were solid at the back. We couldn't get an equaliser and the score finished 1-0 to Chelsea.

I was absolutely gutted to lose. The FA Cup final is the oldest cup competition in the world and I would have loved to have got my hands on the trophy. There is a saying that Wembley is for winners and having experienced both winning and losing, I'd agree with that. We climbed the famous steps to collect our runners up medals and then we stayed on the pitch to watch Chelsea lift the trophy. We applauded our opponents because it had been a hard-fought game and I think it's right to show respect. We were all deflated in the dressing room afterwards and it was very quiet as we reflected on what might have been.

It was the last FA Cup final played at Wembley before it was torn down and replaced with the stadium that we have today, so it was an historic occasion and I was pleased to have been a part of it. After the match, we had a party in London with family and friends as, despite the result, it had still been an achievement to reach the final.

A year later, I received a call from a journalist that I knew asking if I'd seen the new movie *Hannibal* starring Anthony Hopkins.

"No, why?" I replied. I'm not a massive watcher of films.

"Because you're in it!" he said. I didn't believe him, so I got the DVD and watched it and sure enough, in one scene a security guard is watching TV and there I am playing in the FA Cup final on the security guard's screen. I'm only in it for a few moments, but I'm there. It was very strange. I never thought I'd appear in a big Hollywood movie!

My relationship with Gregory deteriorated further during the summer of 2000. When he became manager in 1998, I signed a new contract on the basis that if I had a good year, he would offer me a new one. That following season, I was Villa's top scorer and Player of the Year, so I had stuck to my side of the bargain – Gregory didn't stick to his!

I want to make it clear that none of this was about me being greedy and I wasn't asking for the world. The fact of the matter was that even if I'd been given what I asked for, I'd have still been on a couple or three times less than players like David Ginola and Juan Pablo Angel.

Gregory had messed me around for the entire year. Before the start of the 1999/00 season, I had been in to see him to find out what was happening. He told me to get my agent to give him a call and he'd sort out a new deal. A couple of months later, my agent told me that he couldn't get hold of Gregory, despite leaving several messages.

So I went to see the manager again and he said, "Don't worry, Julian. I'm working on an offer for you. Leave it with me."

Then it went silent again, so I had to hunt him down a month later. "Leave it with me. I just need to run it past the chairman," Gregory said.

Another month went by with no offer forthcoming, so my agent went to see Doug Ellis, the chairman, to see what was going on. Ellis told him that I wouldn't be getting a new deal because I was already under contract.

If Gregory had come up with the goods and stuck to his deal, things could have been different, but by June 2000, I'd had enough and asked for a transfer, even though I didn't want to leave. I was so frustrated, so I said a few things in the papers about Gregory.

This is how Sky Sports reported our bust up:

ASTON VILLA striker Julian Joachim has launched a scathing attack on manager John Gregory, after he stated that 'If I never saw him again, it would be too soon.'

Joachim, 26, asked for a transfer last week after he said that the club reneged on their promise of a new deal at Villa Park.

"That lot could offer me all the money in the world now and it would be too late," said Joachim. "I do not want to kick another ball for Gregory.

"People might have thought that I was making some sort of token stand when I complained about promises not being kept on pay rises, but I wasn't, I'm finished, absolutely finished with John Gregory.

"He has s*** on me, he has not kept his promises and when I dig my heels in I am the most stubborn person in the world, any relationship we had - and we go back a long way - is over.

"What makes me even more angry is that he made sure he sorted himself out with a new £1 million a year, four year contract."

Anyone who knows me will tell you how laid back I am, so for me to speak out like that shows how pissed off I was with the situation.

When we returned for pre-season training, Gregory called me into his office for a showdown. Spread over his desk were all the newspaper cuttings of what I had supposedly said about him.

"What's all this then?" he asked.

I stood up to have a look and went through them individually, "Yes, I said that. No, I didn't say that," and so on. When I had finished, I went to walk out.

"Sit down. I've not finished with you yet," he yelled.

I walked up to him with my finger pointing in his direction and said, "I've fucking had it with you now!"

It was the first time I'd really stood up to Gregory and he didn't like it one bit. He exploded, telling me that he was going to make my life hell. He said he would make me train with the kids, name me as a sub and force me to travel with the squad and he had no intention of ever playing me again.

Within days of our meeting, he took down all the pictures of me from the training ground and around Villa Park, almost like he was trying to erase me from the club.

And we didn't speak at all. We didn't even acknowledge each other if we passed in the corridor. My written transfer request was accepted, although I don't believe Gregory ever had any intention of selling me, I think he wanted to make me suffer.

Our sixth place finish the previous season meant that we had failed to qualify for Europe for the second successive season, but there was another competition, the Intertoto Cup, that took place over the summer months which was a way of qualifying for the UEFA Cup through the back door. Gregory wanted us to enter.

The tournament kicked off mid-July which meant that we had to report for pre-season training much earlier than usual. It was tough when you've had a long hard season like we had as we probably would have benefitted from a longer rest and saved ourselves for the league campaign. We should have been playing pre-season friendlies and trying to get our fitness levels up; instead we were travelling around Europe playing competitive games.

Our first game took place on 16th July 2000 away to Czech side FK Marila Pribram. True to his word, Gregory included me in the squad, dragged me over to the Czech Republic and didn't play me.

When the return leg took place a week later, I found out that the Villa fans had turned against me because the manager had fed stories to the local press saying that I was disrespecting the club and the fans. He named me as a sub and as I took my seat on the bench the boos rang out from the 8,000 home supporters. I found it really upsetting, although I'm sure the manager was loving it!

I couldn't understand why the fans were hammering me because I had done so much for the club, always gave 100% and I hadn't fallen out with them. My comments to the press were about Gregory, not the fans or the club. My issue was with the manager, not the supporters of the club. The Villa fans had always been great to me and I loved them - still do. That is why their reaction hurt me so much.

From behind the dug out I could hear people shouting that I wasn't fit to wear the shirt which saddened me. The abuse got worse when I started to warm up along the touchline; you name it, I was called it. I tried to take it on the chin and ignore it, but it's not easy. I started to panic that Gregory might send me on and when he told me that I was coming on in the 75th minute, I was nervous and wondered how much worse it could get.

When my name was announced over the tannoy, the jeers were deafening and I could hear the venom in the insults that the fans were hurling at me – it was horrendous. It was so bad that when I won a penalty, my own supporters booed me – for winning their side a penalty! We missed the penalty and the fans cheered even more, that's how bad it was.

Our Intertoto campaign ended with defeat to Celta Vigo in the semi-final which was another disapointment in what was becoming my toughest summer as a professional.

When the Premier League season began, we played Chelsea in our first home game and it was awful. I came on in the 70th minute and the boos rang out again. I was jeered every time I touched the ball and couldn't do anything right in the eyes of the supporters. Even if I played a good pass, or took someone on, I still got booed. My mental strength has always been good and I remained resilient and just got on with it. I knew I could win the fans back.

On 23rd September 2000, we were playing Middlesbrough at the Riverside Stadium and I was once again a substitute. Gregory brought me on in the second half and I scored ten minutes after taking to the field. It was a huge relief and I showed the manager that I still had plenty to offer. We drew the game 1-1 and I kept my place on the bench for our next game, a home match against Derby County. As you know, I loved playing against the Rams and that match was when things started to change.

David Ginola got a knock and had to come off early in the first half. The manager sent me on in his place and the inevitable booing began. I was starting to get used to it by then, and although it still wasn't nice, I didn't let it bother me.

Not long after I'd come on, Merse played a great pass to me that I managed to slot into the back of the net. Even though I'd scored for Villa, there were still 20,000 fans booing me and just 5000 cheering. The reaction of my teammates was incredible as they ran towards me to celebrate. They knew what I'd been through and although they could see that I was coping, they knew that it was tough for me. The lads were always brilliant to me and they were a massive help.

Merse grabbed a second for us just before half time and just after the interval, I sent a cross into Alan Wright who netted our third. Chris Riggott pulled one back for Derby, before I grabbed our fourth, three minutes from time.

I was out on the left, took it past two defenders before cutting in and slotting it past Mart Poom in the Derby goal. This time there were 20,000 cheers and only 5000 boos and I could see that I was winning the fans over. To his credit, Gregory knew that I had played well and he took me off with a couple of minutes to go so that the Villa fans could give me a standing ovation which was amazing. I gave them a clap back and it was the turning point for me, the moment I knew that I'd won them back. It was like *Rocky IV* when Rocky travels to Russia to fight Drago, is met with a hostile reception, but eventually wins the crowd over. For that one game, *I* was Rocky Balboa!

I never had, and never have had, a problem with the supporters, the club or the players. My problem was with Gregory and I tried to make that clear to everyone. After the Derby match, my relationship with the manager improved so much that we started to say good morning to each other! We put our differences aside for the sake of the football club because he knew that I had something to offer.

Despite all the off-field problems, I scored seven goals in twenty appearances during the 2000/01 season – just two fewer than our top scorer, Dion Dublin – and we finished eighth in the league.

At the end of the season my time at Villa was over. Gregory called me in to his office and told me that he wanted to sign Mustapha Hadji from Coventry City and that I was going to be part of the deal. Although Coventry had just been relegated to the Championship, I thought that it would be a good move for me. I didn't want to uproot my family as the kids were settled in their schools. Coventry was closer to my house than Birmingham which meant that my family wouldn't be disrupted by the move.

My mate Ian's dad, Jim Blyth, was the goalkeeper coach at Coventry and he told me that they'd come in for me a few times during the season, so I felt wanted which was important to me after everything that I'd just been though. Coventry were managed by Gordon Strachan whom I had met a few times on golfing days and I'd always had a lot of respect for him for what he had achieved as a player, as a manager and how he was as a person.

Obviously, it would have been better to remain in the Premier League, but after my fall out with Gregory I wanted, no needed, a fresh start, so I didn't mind dropping down a division. When I met Gordon to discuss terms, he explained to me that his aim was to get the club back into the Premier League at the first attempt. When I looked at the strength of the Coventry squad, I didn't think we'd have any problem bouncing straight back. We agreed a deal worth £12,000 a week, with goal and appearances bonuses, and I officially became a Coventry City player in July 2001. The move suited all parties and I was looking forward to playing for the Sky Blues and their incredible supporters.

I didn't want to leave anywhere on bad terms – I wasn't that sort of lad – and it was a shame that my five and a half years at Villa ended the way that it did. I always did my best for the club, the fans and my teammates and I hope that the Villa supporters recognise that.

I still follow Villa now and always look out for their results. I sat in the stands with the fans at Wembley to watch the 2019 play off final, signed a few autographs and had my photo taken with the supporters and that was a nice feeling. I'm looking forward to going back to Villa Park again in the future to cheer on the lads now fans are allowed back into the stadiums.

As far as my relationship with John Gregory goes, I haven't seen him since 2001, but I'm still really upset at the way our relationship fell apart. I'm not bitter, just disapointed as I'd known him since I was sixteen, trusted him and wanted to do well for him. I don't think I've ever got over the way that he treated me. If I saw him now I'd shake his hand and say hello, but I wouldn't go out my way to get in touch. It's a real shame.

CHAPTER 13
Sent to Coventry

Introduction by John Eustace. Former Coventry City Captain.

"Jockey was a big signing from Aston Villa, and it was really exciting to have a player of his quality join us. Lee Hughes, another fantastic attacker, came in not long after Julian and their arrivals gave us all a huge lift.

Jockey had a big reputation but had no ego and he was great with the younger lads. He took me under his wing, was very friendly, approachable, and always happy to help.

He came from a big club and we were all keen to see what he was like as a person. We soon realised that he was a good trainer and he instantly became one of the lads.

Going forward he was so dangerous, with his electric pace and he was a good finisher too. As a midfielder, he was exactly the kind of striker that I wanted to play with because I knew he was a hard worker who'd chase every ball. Unfortunately, I suffered a bad knee injury, so I didn't play alongside him as much as I would have liked.

He was well-liked amongst the squad and did generous things for us all the time. He took a group of us to Leicester once, telling us that there was a lovely Chinese restaurant that he knew. We had a great meal and the staff looked after us a treat. When the bill arrived, he said, "Put your money away, lads." We didn't know that it was his restaurant and it was a really nice gesture.

He loved a bet, as did one or two others, and he used to give us all these dodgy tips!"

*****

I was being spoken of as one of Coventry's star signings so there was a lot of pressure on me to perform. There always is when you join a new club, but I was excited and couldn't wait to wear the sky blue shirt and show the fans what I was capable of. I had always enjoyed playing against Coventry City and I was pleased to have joined another big club.

Coventry had enjoyed 34 years in the top division before their relegation at the end of the 2000/01 season. At the time, only Liverpool, Arsenal and Everton had spent more consecutive seasons in the top-flight and the general feeling amongst the players and supporters was that we belonged at the highest level of English football.

Although I felt that we had a great chance of retaining our Premier League status, I was under no illusions as to the difficulties of the task ahead of us. I knew from my time at Leicester that the Championship is a tough, tough league and it wasn't going to be easy to win promotion. In some ways, it is harder for the teams who have just been relegated as they are paying Premier League wages, the supporters are more demanding and other teams raise their game against you. If you don't bounce back quickly – by the second season at the latest – it becomes an even greater challenge.

In Gordon Strachan I felt we had the right man for the task. He told me that he was going to keep our best players and the plan was for me to partner Welsh International John Hartson up front. Hartson was a big, strong target man, who played in a similar style to Dion Dublin and I felt that I could play off him.

But then a month later, there was a mass exodus. Before I signed, strikers Craig Bellamy and John Aloisi had already joined Newcastle and Osasuna respectively, and Mustapha Hadji went to Villa as part of my transfer. Alarm bells started to ring when Hartson was sold to Celtic for £6,000,000. I knew from our few training sessions and pre-season friendlies that we'd have done well together.

We signed Lee Hughes from West Bromwich Albion to replace Hartson. Hughesy was a hard worker and a natural goal scorer, a bit of a poacher. I got on well with him.

Roland Nilsson, a fans' favourite who had enjoyed a successful spell at Coventry between 1997 and 1999, re-joined the club as player-coach. Although Nillson was 37 years of age, he was a vastly experienced defender, a true professional and a nice guy to boot.

By the time the season began with a 1-0 win away at Stockport on 11th August 2001, we had sold six players for a combined £15 million and spent less than £7 million replacing them with five others. There were rumours going around that Coventry were in big trouble financially and the difficult task of promotion suddenly became much harder, especially when our talented goalkeeper, Chris Kirkland, signed for Liverpool for £6 million immediately following the Stockport match. Kirkland was a giant for his age and he looked the part, even though, at just 20 years old, he was very young for a goalkeeper. He was an up and coming keeper and a nice lad too. Marcus Hedman had been our number one, but Chris had been pushing him hard and was expected to become our first choice goalkeeper for years to come.

We signed Andy Goram to be the back-up goalkeeper, another experienced player who had won everything there was to win during his time in Scotland with Rangers. He was another interesting character, in fact, I don't think I've ever met a keeper who I would describe as normal!

I missed the Stockport game, and the next four, because I had injured my ankle ligaments during pre-season. I got back to full fitness and made my debut on 8th September 2001 against Grimsby Town. We played really well; dominating the game with 80% possession and hit the post, the crossbar and Grimsby's keeper pulled off a series of unbelievable saves. You name it, we did it – apart from score. We lost the game 1-0 – our third defeat in four games – and two days later Gordon was sacked.

I couldn't believe it and I wasn't alone in thinking that it was a very harsh sacking. He had been a top class player and had done so well at Coventry, managing on a shoe string budget, keeping Coventry up several times when they had looked doomed. I was looking forward to working with him and then he'd gone after I'd played just one game for him.

I started to wonder what was going on. The country was in the middle of a recession, Coventry were in a financial mess with no money to spend and we were selling our best players. I was worried but didn't have any choice but to knuckle down and hope for the best. I had a job to do for Coventry and was determined to do my best to help turn things around and get us back to where we belonged.

Roland Nilsson was given the job as caretaker manager and I, like most of the players, was delighted for him. He knew the club inside out and deserved the opportunity, without a doubt, even though he lacked managerial experience. He had the respect of the lads and was the perfect fit for us at that time.

Nilsson's first game as caretaker was away at Sheffield United and he hit the ground running, although it was a disaster for me. My ankle flared up again in the second half and I was taken off injured. My replacement, Laurent Delorge, scored the only goal of the game to give us a much-needed three points. That win sparked an eleven-match unbeaten run that saw us climb to the top of the table. Nilsson, quite rightly, was given the job on a permanent basis and won the Manager of the Month award in October 2001.

Unfortunately, I played no part in that fantastic run because of my ankle. For me, there was nothing worse than being injured, especially as I was one of the big signings and there was great expectation on me to perform. The fans were good to me – despite having played for two of their rivals – but I knew that they were frustrated because I was injured so often during those first few months. I shared their frustration and wanted to get back in the line-up as quickly as I could.

Nilsson's honeymoon period came to an abrupt end on 3rd November when we lost to Millwall in the first of six defeats from eight games that saw us tumble down to mid table.

My ankle felt OK when I ran and trained, but I knew that if I rushed back too soon and got caught in a game it would go again, so I had to be patient and accept the five or ten minute cameo appearances from the bench that I made during November and December.

On 23rd December 2001, I got an early Christmas present – my first goal for Coventry. I came off the substitute's bench in the second half of a home game against Bradford City. We were already 3-0 up when I came on and it was one of those games where everything was going to plan. We were playing scintillating football and Bradford couldn't handle us. With ten minutes left to play, David Thompson sent an inviting ball into the box. I controlled it with my right and smashed it in with my left to make it 4-0. It was a huge relief to score and usually once you've got your first, the rest will follow. Unfortunately, I kept picking up niggling injuries that restricted me to just three starts in the second half of the campaign and I didn't score again all season.

It was a turbulent season that saw our chairman, Bryan Richardson, given a vote of no confidence in January 2002 because of the financial problems at the club. Whilst we, the players, tried to distance ourselves from the boardroom politics things were changing all around us and it was a bit unsettling.

On the pitch, our form was mixed, but a victory over Norwich on 9th March 2002 took us up to fourth in the table with seven games to play. We felt that we had a great chance of making the play offs but then it all went wrong.

We picked up just one point from the final seven games and I watched our promotion dreams fall apart whilst I sat in the stands feeling helpless. I wanted to be out there helping the lads, more so when we were struggling because that was when they needed my experience and everything else that I could offer.

We ended up finishing 11th in the league, nine points adrift of the play off places and Nilsson was sacked. I was shocked, but then again, by that stage nothing really surprised me in football anymore. I think he should have been given more time because it was his first season, we were trying to rebuild and he'd been unlucky with injuries to some key players, including me. I think the problem was that people expected us to at least make the play offs, so anything less was deemed not good enough. It's a real shame because he was such a nice bloke. Maybe that was his downfall. I was happy to see Roland win the Swedish League title as manager of Malmo in 2010.

It was a tough first season for me in which I only started six games, made 12 appearances from the bench and scored just one goal. With another new manager coming in, I knew that I was back to square one and would have to prove myself all over again, so I vowed to dedicate the summer to regaining my fitness and I hoped that the new manager would be someone I knew.

It was.

Gary McAllister was the man tasked with leading Coventry back to the Premier League. McAllister had won it all during a glittering playing career that included four seasons at Highfield Road and he came to us as a player-manager which was great, as he was still was a very good player, even though he was by then 37 years old.

I had known Gary Mac since I was a schoolboy trying to earn a YTS contract at Leicester and he was playing in the first team. I liked him immediately. We'd played against each other several times since then and our children attended the same private school, so I used to see him most mornings and say hello.

Eric Black came in to be Gary's assistant and he took the first training session. We did a warm-up and then he got the footballs out for us to play a five a side game, followed by some two touch and we finished with a game of keep ball which showed that they wanted us to play in a passing style.

After training, Gary Mac told us that he wanted us to be a team who were hard to beat and he said that it was a fresh start for everyone. He gained our respect from day one; we all knew that Gary Mac was a winner with bags of experience and he tried to instil a winning mentality within the squad.

Without a doubt the aim was promotion, but it was always going to be difficult because morale was low by then and the club was struggling even more financially.

Gary had worn the number 10 shirt at Leeds and Liverpool and I didn't have any hesitation swapping my squad number from 10 to 8. Some players had clauses in their contracts that stated that they must wear a certain number, but I didn't mind what was on the back of my shirt. The only thing that mattered to me was that I had a shirt.

Despite the turmoil, nothing had really changed for me personally, I was still there to do a job and I remained confident in my ability. We were still a big club with a good side, although we didn't have a lot of squad depth.

We beat Sheffield United 2-1 on the first day of the new campaign and I was delighted to last the full 90 minutes. I started the next three games where we drew to Brighton and beat Reading and Crystal Palace to give us ten points out of a possible 12 which was an excellent start.

And then it all went downhill.

The club's financial situation had worsened and players were being offloaded left, right and centre, for well below their market value as the board sought to bring in as much money as they could. Lee Hughes had been our top scorer in the 2001/02 season and he re-joined West Brom for just £2.5 million, half of what we'd paid for him a year earlier. David Thompson, our Player of the Season, joined Blackburn for just £1.5 million, and our goalkeeper, Magnus Hedman, was sold to Celtic. So, three of our best players were sold and we didn't have any money to bring anyone of the same quality in.

Gary Mac called a team meeting and told us that the situation was so dire that the club might not have the money to see the season out and we were asked if we would be prepared to take a wage deferral. I didn't have any hesitation and so I and a lot of the lads agreed to a 30% deferral.

Things got even worse when I pulled my hamstring following the victory over Palace on 24th August 2002. I remained positive and did plenty of strengthening and speed work in the gym with the physio, building myself back to full fitness. I got back into the squad for a league game against Rotherham and came off the bench to play the final thirty minutes and I felt good, even though I'd needed some injections to get me through it.

But the following week, I suffered a recurrence of an old injury. I couldn't believe it. I had been working so hard. I felt that I was on the mend with regular football on the horizon and then I was back to square one. I hated being injured. Until I joined Coventry, with the exception of my broken foot at Leicester, I had hardly been injured. When I got my second hamstring injury, I began to wonder if all those games that I had played when I was young were catching up with me. I started to ask myself if my body could still cope with the rigours of professional football. It was crazy because I was only 28 and should have been approaching my peak.

While I was out injured, we were inconsistent and our lack of squad depth really cost us. Instead of challenging for promotion, we found ourselves in a relegation battle. The only positives for the club were that we had some promising youngsters coming through the ranks and Gary Mac was prepared to give them a chance.

Gary McSheffrey was a confident young lad who could score all kinds of goals and he made a fantastic start to his career. He was Coventry born and bred and fans love to see local boys progress to the first team so it gave them a big lift.

Callum Davenport was another local lad who made the most of his opportunity. Callum was a tall centre half who read the game well and he became a regular for us during the 2002/03 season.

In January 2003, we were knocked out of the FA Cup by Rochdale which was a huge disappointment. With the side struggling, Gary Mac kept asking me when I'd be coming back and it was good to be able to say soon. The first time that I'd been injured, I'd gone heavy on the weights to try and build the muscle back up, but after the second injury, I decided to lay off the weights and it seemed to work. I made my first start for six months in a 2-0 defeat at home to Bradford on 22nd February 2003 and also started the next five games, scoring two goals.

It was different playing in a side who were in a relegation battle as, apart from one Premier League season with Leicester, I'd only ever known the top end of the table. When the team is playing well, you are confident, and confidence brings luck. When you're struggling, everything seems to go against you.

It felt so good to be playing again, scoring goals after being out for so long and I felt that I'd turned a corner. But even though I was back to full fitness, I soon found myself frozen out.

CHAPTER 14
The Taliban Squad

Introduction by Dean Gordon. Former Coventry City Defender.

"I first met Jockey in 1994 when we were both called up for the England Under 21 team. He was a laid back, shy guy, but a nice lad and someone I had a laugh with. I enjoyed his company, but there was nothing enjoyable about lining up against him!

In the second game of the 1998/99 season, I was playing for Middlesborough against Aston Villa and he caused me quite a few problems. I was more of a left back really, but I had been moved to centre back for that game and I was up against Jockey. He was a fast, skilful player, with a short, stocky build, which made him difficult to deal with. I was strong and quick and while we had a good battle, he did get the better of me a few times. He scored after six minutes and with 15 minutes to go, we were 2-1 down, chasing an equaliser when Jockey got the ball and tried to go past me. I managed to get my arm in to stop him and I won the ball, but he tumbled to the ground and the ref gave Villa a free kick. It was never a foul and I remember that I was annoyed with him because he'd gone down too easily. They scored from the free kick and as Jockey ran past me, he turned, laughed and gave me a look that said, "I've done you there, mate!" Next time I see him, I'll remind him of that!

I played against him a few times over the years and always did ok, but he was a tough opponent and I much preferred having him on my team.

When I joined Coventry in 2002, I roomed with Jockey which was nice as we got on well and we had some good conversations. We've kept in touch since our careers ended which is rare in football.

Julian was able to overcome some big challenges at Coventry which didn't surprise me because he was so resilient. You have to have a little bit extra in you to reach the Premier League and to play at the level that he had for so long. Top-flight football is not for the faint hearted; physically it's tough and mentally it's tough. That is why players give each other so much respect because we know how hard it is. You need character to do what Jockey did and I'm not surprised that he bounced back from tough times because he is that sort of person. Jockey is one of those people who, when they are written off, goes the extra mile to prove people wrong."

*****

By the end of March 2003, we were mathematically safe from relegation and Gary Mac called a team meeting.

"Now that we have avoided the drop, I'm looking towards next season. I've made up my mind on who is and who isn't in my plans and for the remaining eight matches, I'm only going to play those who will be involved next year," he told us.

We were called in to see him individually and he broke the news to me that I wasn't in his plans. He told me to ask my agent to get in touch with him so that they could arrange a pay off for me. I was shocked because I had finally got back to full fitness and was playing well. I didn't want to leave, but when the manager tells you you're not wanted, you have no choice, so I called my agent and explained what had happened.

My agent rang Gary Mac and while I don't know exactly what was said, I do know that the chat didn't go well. The club had no money, so they couldn't afford to pay me off, so I turned up for training the following day as usual. Eric Black came over and told those of us who weren't in the gaffer's plans to train separately, away from the rest of the senior players.

Even during my difficult season at Villa, I had still been part of the squad and amongst the lads, so it was a whole new experience being frozen out. I didn't like it, but at least I wasn't alone. There were nine of us in the same situation, including Youssef Chippo and John Eustace. All we could do was to get our heads down, work hard and try and convince the manager to give us another chance.

A few days later, Gary Mac called me into his office to tell me that Sheffield Wednesday had made an offer to take me on loan for the last six games of the season. Wednesday were a big club, but they were pretty much doomed and I didn't want to go there and get a relegation on my CV. It would look like I'd helped take them down and I didn't want that, so I said no. He wasn't happy.

The following day, I was called into his office again. "I've had Danny Wilson on the phone. He wants to take you to Bristol City for the rest of the season. They are in League One and challenging for promotion," McAllister said.

"Sorry, gaffer," I replied. "I'm not going to Bristol to live in a hotel away from my family if I'm only going to play for six games."

He had the right hump with me because he wanted me off the wage bill, but I wasn't going to be forced out of the club. Later that day, Eric Black came over to me and told me that the manager wanted me in for an 8 a.m. start the next day, a couple of hours earlier than normal.

So, I arrived at the training ground at 7.30 a.m. because we always had to be there thirty minutes before we began. No one else was there. Eric finally arrived at 9 a.m. and told me to get changed and meet him on the training pitch. He then instructed me to run around the perimeter until he told me to stop. After an hour and a quarter, he called me in and told me to grab a shower, get my kit back on and return to the pitch for 10:30 a.m. when he instructed me to run around the perimeter again until noon!

As I trudged back to the dressing room, he told me to have another shower, eat some lunch and to meet him outside again at 2 p.m. where he had me doing sprints for an hour, again on my own. When I finished that, he said, "Same time tomorrow."

I wasn't having that, so when I got home I was straight on the phone to my agent. He phoned the PFA because Coventry had breached all kinds of rules. You're not supposed to make players train on their own for starters. The PFA rang the club and then I got a call to tell me that I'd be training with the first team again the next day. 'Great, this is my chance to get back into the fold,' I thought to myself.

So I arrived at training the next day and we started with a bit of keep ball which is where the players form a circle with two lads in the middle who have to try and win the ball from those on the outside. If they tackle you or intercept your pass, then you take their place in the middle. You're only allowed two touches and it's a good way to warm up.

One of the players in the middle was McAllister. The ball came to me and I passed it to a teammate with my first touch. I'm not kidding, after at least a second after I'd played it, Gary Mac came in, studs up and took a chunk out of my shin. I'm convinced it was deliberate, but Gary apologised and claimed it was an accident. He started to feign concern and asked me how I was.

"Fine," I replied. I had been taught not to show when I was hurt.

I think that he was waiting for me to react so that he could kick me out of the club without having to pay me a penny. There was no way I was going to give him the satisfaction, so I just had to get on with it and not let it get me down. It was a good job that I was strong enough to cope mentally.

The worst part for me was that the situation affected my kids. They were still attending the same school as McAllister's son and I think some of the children at the school made some nasty comments to my kids. It's one thing treating me like that, I was still getting paid, but it was nothing to do with my children and wasn't fair on them. They were coming home from school in tears. I wasn't having that, although I know it wasn't Gary's fault that my kids were brought into it.

By this time Coventry's debts had amassed to a staggering amount, £20 million was being reported, and I had been taking a 30% wage deferral for almost year, with no complaints because I was happy to do so. I didn't deserve the treatment that I was receiving; the club had told me that they didn't want me, tried to force me out on loan and then started playing these silly games. Enough was enough. I phoned my agent and told him to contact the club and tell them that I wanted all the money that they owed me immediately and that they could also start paying me 100% of my wages again. They reluctantly paid me back in three instalments. It wasn't about the money, it was the principle.

When I reported for pre-season training in July 2003, myself and the rest of the outcasts were made to train on a park in Coventry, while the rest of the squad were training at Warwick University. We became known as the Taliban Squad!

I just got on with it. I had no choice. I was in the final year of my contract and I wanted to stay fit and impress in friendlies and reserve team matches to put myself in the shop window so that another club would sign me. I still enjoyed playing football and felt that I could still offer the club something if only I was given the chance.

Towards the end of September, we were sitting in 20th position and McAllister was under a lot of pressure. He'd changed the squad quite drastically during the summer and the board were expecting immediate results. He knew that he needed to do something different, so he called me in to his office and told me that the coaches had said that I was working really hard and he wanted to bring me back into the first team squad.

"Look, Julian," he began. "I need to speak to the chairman and the board, but I want you back in the squad. You look fit and sharp, and I need your experience. But if I do play you, we can't afford to pay you your appearance fee."

"I'm no good to anyone sitting on the side-lines, gaffer. I just want to play, so I'm willing to waive my appearance fee," I replied My appearance fee was worth £2500 a game, so it was a lot of money, but I was a footballer and just wanted to play football.

"That's good to hear. I'll speak to the board and see if they are happy," McAllister said.

And that was it, I was involved again. It just goes to show how quickly things can change in football. I wasn't happy with the way that I had been treated – I'm still not happy – but I never gave less than 100%.

On 1st October 2003, we were playing Crewe at home and I was on the substitutes' bench wearing the number 21 shirt. Patrick Suffo had taken my number eight in the summer when no one had expected me to play for the club again. It was the first time that I had been in the squad for six months and I was desperate to get on and play a competitive game again. I got my wish at half time when I replaced Dele Adebola and I made my mark immediately.

Within two minutes of taking to the field, I crossed the ball into McAllister who headed us in front. Andy Morrell added a second for us with 15 minutes left on the clock to give us a vital three points.

I've already mentioned that I liked to read the sports sections of the newspapers and it was really pleasing to read this article in *The Guardian* the following day.

"Julian Joachim's chances of earning a reprieve at Highfield Road were given a boost last night after the transfer-listed forward's impressive second-half performance helped clinch what was only Coventry's second home league win during 2003.

Joachim has agreed to sacrifice his appearance bonuses in an attempt to win back the affections of Gary McAllister and he may have succeeded following his efforts in creating the player-manager's opening goal.

The diminutive striker was deemed surplus to requirements by McAllister in the summer as one of the club's highest earners. But last night his energetic appearance as a substitute invigorated his team's lacklustre display and his sublime cross led to McAllister's simple header.

"Julian gave us a spark and he has now shown me that he still wants to play for this football club," said McAllister. "He has agreed to waive his appearance bonuses, which is a substantial amount of money, but that just shows what he is about.

"All credit to the guy because he's been determined to remain a Coventry player. If he can keep his concentration he could be an important part of our season."

I scored my first and second goals of the season against Gillingham on 22nd November in just my second start of the season and that was that. I was back in the fold and stayed there for the rest of the season. It was a huge turnaround; six months earlier I was deemed surplus to requirements, but I ended up playing the best football of my time at Coventry. My resilience and hard work paid off.

On 12th December 2003, Gary McAllister temporarily stood down as player-manager for family reasons. On a personal level, I was saddened for Gary, but professionally, I was looking forward to a fresh start under a new manager.

Eric Black, McAllister's assistant, was given the job as caretaker and I was pleased. Despite the punishing training session that he conducted when things turned sour, I got on well with Eric and I wanted to play for him.

In January 2004, McAllister resigned and Black was given the job on a permanent basis. He couldn't have got off to a better start when we beat Walsall 6-1 at the Bescott Stadium. I scored our fourth goal. Gary McSheffrey put me through and I rolled back the years, sprinting at the defender before smashing home from just outside the area. That win sent us up to 14th in the table to give us an outside chance of making the play offs. By 17th March, we were tenth in the league.

But we lacked consistency and only won one of our next seven games which ended our promotion hopes. We ended that dismal run with a fantastic 5-2 victory away at Gillingham.

We were 17th when Eric took over and he had us playing some good stuff and then out of the blue, just after the Gillingham game, he was sacked! We finished 12th that season, just eight points away from a play off spot, so there had been progress, but the board decided that they wanted to go with someone with more experience.

Former England international Peter Reid came in to be our fifth manager in three seasons. He seemed alright, but I didn't get a chance to play for him because my contract was up at the end of the season. He offered me a new deal of £3,000 a week, way short of the £12,000 that I had been earning and I turned it down. But it wasn't about the money, my decision to waive my appearance fee proved that as it ended up costing me about £80,000. I chose to leave because after everything I had been through I thought that a fresh start would be best for me.

When I look back on my three years at Highfield Road, I try to forget the injury plagued first two and instead, focus on that final season where I played 32 games, scored 11 times and finished just one goal behind our top scorer, Gary McSheffrey. I'm incredibly thankful that I had that last year so that I could show the Coventry fans what I could do. They were always great towards me and I hope they appreciate that I always gave my all every time I wore the sky blue shirt.

Sadly, Coventry City's financial situation got worse and the I was saddened to watch the club tumble down the leagues and be forced to play their 'home' games at Northampton and Birmingham's grounds. I think my old teammate, Mark Robins, is doing a fantastic job and I hope it won't be long before they are back in the Premier League.

CHAPTER 15
Dressing room rows and naked table tennis

Introduction by Brian Deane. Former Leeds United striker.

I was born in Leeds and had spent four years at Elland Road during the nineties, so when I was offered the chance to return to the club in July 2004, I felt that it was the ideal move for me. Another new signing for Leeds that summer was Julian Joachim, a player that I had played against a few times when he was at Leicester and Aston Villa. I had also watched Julian star for England in the Under 18 European Championships, so I knew what his strengths were and I was intrigued at the prospect of playing alongside him.

He reminded me a lot of my good friend, Franz Carr, with his direct style of play and his speed, but Julian was a finisher too. I knew that his pace and experience would cause problems in the Championship and he gave the manager a different option. At that time, we also had Aaron Lennon in the squad who was another extremely quick player.

I played for a host of clubs throughout my career and always liked playing with good players and Julian was very good. I enjoyed having him as my strike partner, although we didn't play together too often. I remember one game against Plymouth and, even though he didn't score, he ran their defence ragged and looked like he was really enjoying himself.

Off the pitch, Julian was very quiet, but he had a very unique way of announcing himself at 9.30 a.m. each morning by walking into the changing room and farting! We'd be sitting in the dressing room getting ready for training and when he walked through the door I'd think, 'here he comes again!' Right on cue, he'd let one out and give us all a flavour of him! It's not like he was subtle about it either, it was like he was shouting from the rooftops!

Other than that, Julian was a good person and a great teammate.

*****

I didn't have to wait long to find a new club and it was a huge one.

Just three years after reaching the Champions League semi-final, Leeds United were relegated from the Premier League. The club were suffering a financial crisis which meant that they were looking to sign experienced players on free transfers who could help them bounce back to the Premier League. Erik Black recommended me to Kevin Blackwell, who had just been appointed as the new Leeds manager, and Blackwell got in touch. As soon as I heard that Leeds had come in for me, I signed straight away. The club had debts of over £100 million, so I knew that I'd have to take a big pay cut. But it wasn't about the money, Leeds were a great club, with a rich history and a large fan base. It was a no brainer.

I signed a two-year deal on £3,500 a week, a big drop from the money I had been earning at Coventry. I know that is still a very good wage, but a footballer's career is short, and you have to earn as much money as you can, as quickly as possible. There aren't many jobs where you take a 70% pay cut. One minute you're at the top, earning good money and the next minute you're dropping down the divisions and your wages reduce accordingly. Although I might have been able to get more money elsewhere, this was a big opportunity for me to play for a massive club.

It was a fresh start for me and my family as we uprooted and moved to Leeds to be closer to the training ground. It was a difficult decision as I'd lived in Leicester since I was 16 and the move meant new schools for the children, but my family were always supportive of me and we all agreed that it was the right thing to do.

I was hoping that we could challenge for promotion, but I knew it would be a massive undertaking because there were so many changes around the club. England internationals, Paul Robinson and Alan Smith, had already departed before I joined and Blackwell told me that more big names would be following them out of the door before the season started.

Sure enough, within a month James Milner, Mark Viduka, Ian Harte, Nick Barmby, Dominic Matteo and Danny Mills had left. They were all either full or Under 21 international players, so I knew that we were weakening as a squad, but Blackwell was bringing in lots of other lads to freshen things up.

I was Blackwell's first signing and was soon followed by Michael Ricketts, Jermaine Wright, Matthew Spring, Brian Deane, Neil Sullivan, Steve Guppy, David Healy, Craig Hignett and Danny Cadamarteri – all experienced pros who, more importantly from Leeds' perspective, didn't cost the club a penny. It was Kevin Blackwell's first managerial role, so it really was a whole new team and we'd need time to gel.

But despite the departure, we still had a lot of quality players who decided to stay at Elland Road.

Gary Kelly was our right back and had been at Leeds forever. He was a good trainer with bags of experience, was well liked by all and wanted the best thing for the club. We had a lot of young players coming through and Gary was a good role model for them.

Lucas Radebe was our captain. A South African international defender and another crowd favourite. He was a credit to Leeds, and I could see why he is considered a club legend. He was also a really nice bloke who helped me to settle in when I joined.

In goal we had a young keeper called Scott Carson. He was a good honest lad who at times was unbeatable in training. Although he was very quiet, you could see that he was destined for bigger things. By January he had been snapped up by Liverpool. It was a great move for him and he won a Champions League winners' medal at the end of that same season.

Another promising youngster was Aaron Lennon who burst onto the scene and became one of our star players during the 2004/05 season. He was quick with an eye for goal and he reminded me a bit of myself in my younger days. He was a nice lad too and we knew that he wouldn't stay at Leeds for long, especially as the manager was under pressure to balance the books. Kelly and Lennon were fast, but even at 29 I was still up there with the quickest in the squad.

Our first game of the season was a 1-0 win over Derby County. I started which was good and it showed me that I was going to be given the opportunity to prove myself. I had a couple of chances to score before Frazer Richardson scored the only goal of the game.

I scored my first Leeds goal on 11th September against my former club, Coventry, at Elland Road. It was a poacher's goal from inside the six-yard box and it was a huge relief to get off the mark. The first goal for a new club was always so important for me.

I was hoping that goal was going to be the first of many, but I was in and out of the team throughout my time at Leeds, more out than in in reality. There was so much competition up front and I wasn't always at my best so I can't really argue that I didn't start too often.

The results weren't great because we didn't have the consistency that would have come from having a settled side. There were too many players coming in and going out which made Blackwell's job hard. He was a decent manager and I got on well with him, although we did have one big fall out.

Dressing room rows are a lot more common than most fans realise. The high-profile cases will make the papers, like the time that Sir Alex Ferguson was reported to have kicked a boot at David Beckham, but most incidents are never made public. At times it doesn't take much for people to fall out at half- or full-time because there are so many emotions going around and players are pumped up anyway from the game. In the main, the fall outs are a way for players to get their frustrations out and 90% of the time you have a chat afterwards, move on, and that's it. Some players will take criticism, others will become defensive before pumping their chests out and raising their voices. It won't surprise you that I used to sit quietly and take the criticism directed at me. Until it got too much, that is.

I felt that Blackwell had been on my case quite a lot throughout the season. He would bring things up after a game and have a little pop at me and because I was quiet, I just sat there and didn't bite. I tried not to let it get to me, but it was happening more frequently and eventually I had enough and stood up to him.

I can't remember who we were playing, but after one home game things were getting quite heated in the dressing room. Blackwell's assistant, Big Sam Ellis, was shouting at a couple of players, while others were arguing amongst themselves. The gaffer hadn't said a word yet and was letting Ellis get on with it. The tensions were escalating and as usual I was sitting there with my head down, trying not to get involved. When I did happen to look up, I could see out of the corner of my eye that Blackwell was watching me and I thought, 'he's coming for me.' I was ready for him.

Blackwell stepped in and told everyone to shut up so that he could have his say. The lads quietened down and he walked towards me, finger pointing, and he began to give me a bollocking about a situation from the game where he felt I should have done better. I sprung out of my seat and yelled, "Shut the fuck up, you knob. Step outside and I'll fucking knock you out."

I completely lost my head. It wasn't like me at all, but I felt he'd taken it too far. No one likes to be told off and I'd always taken the easy route and avoided confrontation but enough was enough, I wanted to fight my corner. I walked towards him and the dressing room was silent, you could hear a pin drop. No one expected me to react like that and the lads were watching on to see what was going to happen.

"That's more like it, Jockey," the gaffer said. "That's what I wanted to see, more fight from you." I'm not sure if that was Blackwell's way of diffusing the situation or whether it was a managerial masterstroke, but it certainly eased the tension.

"Yeah, you fucking knob," a few of the lads said as they started taking the piss, laughing and joking. I think they were pleased that I'd stood up for myself.

Even our coach, Aidy Boothroyd, put his arm around me as I was walking out of the dressing room and said, "Well done, that was a long time coming."

Blackwell called me into his office on the Monday morning and was great with me. "I want to see more of that from you on the pitch," he said. "You're in my plans and I think you've got more in you. That's why I was having a go at you."

After that he was as good as gold. There were times where I hadn't played well and he was praising me – it was one extreme to the next. I felt loved again and it was great to get things off my chest. These incidents are all part and parcel of football.

Even though we were struggling on the pitch, the fans were amazing. Elland Road was packed out for most games, the supporters were the main constant and they love their football. I'm so pleased that Leeds are now back in the Premier League where they belong.

I scored my second Leeds goal on Boxing Day, the winner against Sunderland. It was another poacher's goal and a great Christmas present for me. I felt that I was starting to find some form, but then I got injured again.

We were playing Derby at Pride Park, a team that I had always enjoyed playing against, and I was in full flow with the ball when I felt my hamstring go. It was a bad tear and I was out for around 10 weeks. At some clubs, they try force you to have injections so that they can rush you back – like McGhee had done when I was at Leicester – but at Leeds they did things the right way. There was no cutting corners and the physios put together a comprehensive rehab. plan with milestones that needed to be met before I could move on to the next stage. I remained patient and eventually played a few reserve games, scoring a couple of times too. Blackwell got me involved with the first team again and that's when one of my old teammates got in touch.

It was transfer deadline day in March 2005 when Kevin Blackwell called me in and told me that Paul Merson wanted me to join him in League One for Walsall, on loan until the end of the season. Merse had heard that I was coming back from injury and he needed some firepower as Walsall were deep in a relegation battle. I wasn't in the starting line-up at Leeds and needed game time and Merse saw an opportunity for us to help each other out.

"While you are still a part of my squad, I can't guarantee you first team football. Do you want to go?" Blackwell asked me.

"I need to get my fitness up and I'd rather play first team football than reserves, so yes, I'll go," I replied.

"That's a good attitude to have," Blackwell said. "I'll ring Merson back and ask him to contact you."

Merse called me almost immediately and said, "Jockey, I could do with some help. We are hovering above the relegation zone, but we play some good football and I know you'll do well for us."

My family were settled in Leeds and I didn't want to disrupt them for a loan spell, so Merse agreed that I could travel down to Walsall on a Wednesday night, train Thursday and Friday, play on a Saturday and then go back home to Leeds. It sounded good to me and I signed.

Walsall was a nice little club with a great set of lads who helped me to settle in. I knew Merse well from our time at Villa, of course, and it was good to team up with him again, although I never got the hang of calling him gaffer – it was always Merse! We both liked a bet, and we'd often ask each other how we'd got on and tell each other one or two stories about some decent horses that had won us a few quid.

Merse was a good boss who had the respect of the lads because of who he was and what he'd achieved in the game. If we won, he'd give us a couple of days off which was great.

Even though we were struggling in the league, the atmosphere was fantastic and morale was pretty high. We had some table tennis tables at the training ground and before we trained, the lads would have a few games of 'best of eleven'. There was a rule that if you lost 6-0, you had to run around the training pitch naked! They were the rules and you knew what you were getting into when you picked up the bat. One morning I was playing against Merse and I was 5-0 down. I'll be honest here, I was shitting it. Fortunately, I managed to win the next point and avoid the humiliation. One or two others weren't so lucky, though. It was all a bit of fun and helped to boost the team spirit.

I scored in my second game for Walsall, a 3-2 loss at Barnsley. We were 19th in the table and hadn't won for eight games, but that was all about to change.

We drew to Torquay on 2nd April and beat Peterborough 2-0 the following week before playing Hull City off the park in a 3-0 win. At the time Hull were flying and vying for the league title, but we were too strong for them. It was a memorable game for me as I scored all three goals, the first hat trick of my professional career. What made it even more special was that it was the perfect hat trick – one with my head, one with my left and one with my right.

I scored in our next game too, a 3-1 win against fifth place Hartlepool and then we won the final game of the season 3-0 at home to Stockport to finish the season in a very comfortable 14th place. We played proper football and there is no doubt in my mind that if there were more games remaining, we'd have made the play offs.

After the Stockport game I said my goodbyes to the lads. I loved my short time at Walsall, it gave me the belief that I could still score goals. Five goals in eight games endeared me to the fans too and Merse told me that he was interested in signing me permanently. I still had a year left on my Leeds contract and as I went on my summer holiday, I didn't have a clue where I was going to end up next season.

I returned to Thorp Arch, Leeds United's training ground, in late June 2005 ready to begin pre-season training. I felt fit, sharp and raring to go for the season ahead. Kevin Blackwell had been impressed with my performances at Walsall and had told me that he wanted me to be part of his squad to challenge for promotion to the Premier League.

Walsall tried to sign me on a permanent deal, but it didn't feel right and we weren't able to agree terms. Then at the start of July, Blackwell called me into his office and told me about another offer that he'd received – one that I was definitely interested in.

"I've just had Steve Evans, Boston United's manager, on the phone. He wants to take you to York Street. I've told him that you wouldn't be interested because they are in League Two and you're better than that level."

I didn't really want to drop down two divisions, but then again, it was Boston, my hometown club. As a young kid, I'd go with my friends to watch Boston play non-league football and I suddenly felt excited about the prospect of playing in front of my friends and family. My mum and all the people I'd grown up with still lived in Boston and the more I thought about it, the more I began to see it as a good opportunity to go home.

"Actually, gaffer, I might be interested," I replied.

"Really? I can't guarantee you will be starting every game, but you are an important member of my squad, so don't rush into anything. I don't want you to go, but I won't stand in your way," he said. Blackwell had spent six years as Boston's goalkeeper in the eighties and he knew it was a nice little club.

I met up with Steve Evans and had a chat. Boston had a rich non-league history, turning fully professional as late as 2001 and winning promotion to the football league the following season.

Paul Gascoigne had played 10 games for Boston during the 2004/05 season and Steve told me that he thought my arrival would give the lads and the supporters a similar lift. Evan's expectations for Boston were to finish in the top half and maybe push for a play off spot. I liked Steve instantly and my decision was made there and then – I was going to join Boston.

The move didn't make sense financially as I would have to take a 50% pay cut.

It wasn't a football decision either. I was still only 30 and felt that I could still perform at a decent level – the move to Walsall proved that I could still do it – and if it was anyone other than Boston, I would have turned them down.

I was going home.

CHAPTER 16
Boston bound

Introduction by Lawrie Dudfield. Former Boston United Striker.

"When Jockey signed for Boston, he had a few days off before he joined up with the rest of us. The lads were excited that we had signed someone of Julian's calibre and we were asking each other what kind of car he'd be driving. A few of us were even taking bets. Will he arrive in a Porsche? A Ferrari? Maybe a Maserati?

Then, on the day of his arrival, this old, shitty, clapped out, big, white 12-seater van, with rust on both sides, pulled into the car park. We thought that it was a delivery driver or a contractor, but no. It was Premier League star, Julian Joachim, our big-name signing! The boys were on the floor, crying with laughter when he stepped out of the van. Nobody expected it at all. But that was Julian, he wasn't bothered. He didn't care, he didn't need to arrive in a flash motor, he was like, this is what I've got, this is who I am. It was a great leveller for the boys. No-one was sure what he'd be like as a player or a person, but we knew in that instant that he'd fit in straight away. That story really sums Julian up.

I was surprised that he chose to drop down a couple of divisions to join us, but when I got to know him I realised that he was a great, very modest guy who just loves playing football. It's one thing going down a level, but it's another thing to perform. A lot of people think it's easier, but it's actually harder, because he wasn't surrounded with the quality that he was used to. Jockey just got on with it and worked as hard as anyone when he was on the field, which is all credit to him.

He was brilliant as a player and a person. I am a football geek and he doesn't know this, I never told him, but I wrote to him when

I was a kid asking for a signed picture which I still have to this day. So for me to be playing up front with Jason Lee, Noel Whelan and Julian Joachim – all these ex-Premier League stars, was quite an experience.

In terms of Jockey, he was absolutely rapid and was amazing to play alongside. He was great for me, passing on his experience which was a big help. He was also a calming presence for me. I didn't know where my career was going at that time and Jockey and Jason made things easier for me.

Julian was a Premier League striker playing down at League Two. When he wanted to, he still had that Premier League ability. At times his hamstrings held him back, but on his day, he was the best player in the league by an absolute mile."

✱✱✱✱✱

Kate, the kids and I all decided to leave our house in Leeds and move to Boston which was lovely as we were able to see more of my mum and the rest of my family. I'd left home at 16 and had only seen my friends and family now and again and I'd missed out on a lot. It was the right time for me to go back.

I knew it was going to be a new challenge, working in a totally different environment. We didn't have a training ground for a start. We trained here, there and everywhere, often in public parks. It didn't really matter where, as long as we had a bit of grass to train on, but I didn't mind at all and just got on with it. It showed me how spoilt I'd been previously.

I think the fans and the lads got a bit of a buzz from my arrival. I knew that I'd been at bigger clubs than most of my new teammates and I was probably going to be one of the better players in the team, but you could never accuse me of being big time. I'm far from that. I got on well with my new teammates who were a great bunch of lads and we had some laughs.

Jason Lee was a big, strong striker who had made his name playing for Nottingham Forest in the Premier League. Although, like me, he was coming to the end of his career, he was still a good player who knew where the goal was. Jason was very vocal on the pitch and in the dressing room, and he had a big influence over the younger lads. He was a very physical player, who loved a battle – defenders knew that they'd been in a game when they played against him. I loved playing up front with him. When the ball was in the air, he'd go up – elbows out like the old-school strikers back in the day – and, more often than not, win the ball and flick it on to me. Jason was well respected, and rightly so. He went on to manage the club a few years later.

Another striker in the ranks was Lawrie Dudfield, a very good player who was big, strong and quick. His fitness levels were amazing and he was a good finisher too. I felt that Lawrie was an under-rated player throughout a career where he played for several teams, including Leicester City, Northampton, Hull City and Notts County.

I also linked up again with Noel Whelan, a new signing from Aberdeen, and someone I hadn't played with since 1993, when we were both members of the squad that won the Under 18 European Championships. Back then we were a couple of wide-eyed kids, at the beginning of our journey and now we were both nearing the end. It was a stark reminder that time waits for no man and it made me even more determined to make the best of what was left of my career.

Paul Ellender was our captain. A club legend, Paul had been with Boston since their non-league days and now has a restaurant at Boston's new stadium named after him. Not many people can say that!

Steve Evans, the gaffer, was in his second spell as manager of Boston, but still very much learning his trade. He is one of football's good guys, a real character who was keen for me to share my knowledge with him. He'd call me into his office most mornings for a chat, asking how the different managers I had played under would have handled certain situations. I'd say, he'd probably do this or that, but I was second guessing really. Evans treated me like one of his mates, rather than one of his players and we got on well. He's gone on to have a good career in management.

When I made my Boston debut against Wrexham on 6th August 2005, I discovered just how tough the division was. People may think that if you're used to playing in the Premier League then League Two must be easier. It's actually the opposite. The better the players around you, the easier it is. The further you go down the leagues, the harder I found it. The level and standards drop massively. I'd previously played alongside great talents like Mark Draper, David Beckham and Paul Merson, all players who were capable of spotting my runs and passing the ball to exactly where I wanted it. You don't get that in the lower leagues, so I had to work much harder.

The majority of defenders who I came across in League Two were big, strong and in my face all the time. The quality wasn't the same – it was still a decent standard, but once you've played at the highest level you can instantly see the difference.

I made my home debut against Stockport County in front of a crowd of just 2,432 – 12 months earlier I'd been playing in front of 34,000 for Leeds at Elland Road. The grounds may have been different, but the game of football was still the same and I just did what I'd always done. Five minutes into the second half, I scored my first Boston goal, latching on to the end of a pass from David Noble and flicking it over the keeper. Stockport hit back, scoring two goals in three minutes before I scored an equaliser in the last minute to snatch a draw.

After the game, Evans told the media that I was the best striker in the division. Even though I was in the twilight of my career, I still enjoyed hearing people say nice things about me.

It was great to get off the mark early doors and the goals kept flowing for me.

One of my best performances of the season came in November. It was the first round of the FA Cup and we faced Swindon Town who were in the division above. I scored two and set up the other two in a 4-1 win. Swindon's goalkeeper for that match was future England international, Tom Heaton, who was on loan from Manchester United.

I scored another brace a week later at home to promotion-chasing Wrexham. After the game, Evans told the press, "Joachim was class and he should be playing at Championship level at least. He was the clear difference between the sides and every time we got the ball to him I don't think Wrexham got near him."

David Tuttle, the manager of Championship side, Millwall, must have been listening because as soon as the transfer window opened in January, he put in a bid for me. Evans had no intention of selling me though and the offer was rejected. I was happy at Boston, enjoying my football and I didn't want to leave.

Our league form was decent, and we were exceeding expectations, pushing for a play off place. We would have been higher up the league if we had been able to score penalties, but a succession of misses from 12 yards had cost us some valuable points.

I'd never taken a spot kick during my professional career. Most people thought that I'd want to take penalties because I was a striker, and it was a way of getting your numbers up, but I couldn't think of anything worse. Well, other than giving a post-match interview! Taking a penalty in front of the crowd, with all that time to play mind games with yourself – no thanks.

On 21st January 2006, we were sitting in the dressing room, getting ready to play Bury in an important league match, when Evans asked, "Who's on pens today?" Several hands shot up – none of which were mine – and he looked around before saying, "Jockey, you're taking penalties today."

Please don't get one today, was my immediate reaction! It was in my head as we ran out on to the pitch. Throughout the warm-up I was thinking, 'don't get a penalty. Don't get a penalty.' I was so nervous, but the nerves vanished once the game kicked off and my mind was focussed on the task ahead.

I gave us the lead after 26 minutes and was playing well. And then disaster – the referee gave us a penalty. 'Oh shit,' I thought. It was sod's law that we'd get one and the pressure was right on now. I hung back, waiting for someone else to pick up the ball and take the spot kick, but no one did. So I placed the ball on the penalty spot and took a few steps back.

People think you should score pens all day long as a striker and maybe you should. But it's not just about kicking the ball, it's the mental side that make penalties hard. During the game, it's all instinctive and I always found that the longer I had to think about what I was going to do, the tougher it was. One on ones are hard when you've run 30 or 40 yards, the defenders are chasing you and you only have the keeper to beat. You've got all that time to think about it and by the time you've considered all the options, your mind is tied up in knots and you've missed. That is what penalties are like. They are much harder than they look.

So as I stood twelve yards away from goal, waiting for the referee to blow his whistle, I began to go through the options in my head and totally over complicated the task ahead of me. Shall I go left or right? Or maybe straight down the middle? Do I place it or go for power?

I took a deep breath, ran up to the ball, hit it with my right foot and slipped, like John Terry did in the 2008 Champions League final. Luckily for me, the ball went in, but I could quite easily have missed, like Terry did. I've already explained the amazing buzz that I felt when I scored a goal. This one was completely different, I didn't feel joy, just relief. I never took another penalty after that one, so at least I can say I've got a 100% record in spot kicks!

I genuinely believe that we were only a player or two away from being considered genuine promotion contenders. Our home form was pretty good, it was our results on the road that cost us. We took just 21 points from our travels, the same amount as Oxford United who were relegated, and scored just 16 goals away from home which was the lowest in the division. At the end of the season we finished in 11th place, just five points away from the play off places which shows how close we were. It was, and remains, the highest league finish in Boston's history, so it was a big achievement. I really enjoyed the season, playing week in, week out, and I was Boston's top scorer with 16 goals. Well, 17 actually, as my old teammate Lawrie Dudfield explains:

"I have 100%, definitely stolen one of Jockey's goals. We drew 1-1 away at Bury in September 2005. Our equaliser was a goal mouth scramble. I wasn't even near the ball and the goal was credited to me. I'm not even convinced that I had the second to last touch either. It was Julian's goal, but he's never even mentioned it to me since, even though he must know that he put it in the net! Goals were everything to everyone else, but he wasn't even bothered about it! After the game I was interviewed and asked to talk them through 'my goal' which was awkward as it didn't even come off me. Mind you, Julian scored a lot more goals than me in his career, so I suppose it was OK for me to claim one!"

At the end of the 2005/06 season, it was clear that Boston were in a mess financially. Fortunately, I was still being paid because the club had arranged a sponsor who would cover my wages if there was a problem.

Boston were under pressure to cut back which resulted in a mass exodus, not just of players, but also our chairman Jon Sotnik who joined Darlington's board. I'm not sure of the ins and outs, but Sotnik had loaned Boston some money and as part of the loan, it was agreed that Darlington would have the first option on me if I was ever put up for sale.

There were lots of rumours about me leaving the club as I was one of the few players who could command a transfer fee, so for the third successive year, I went away on my summer holiday in limbo, wondering where I would be playing the following season.

CHAPTER 17
An unwanted man

Introduction by Tommy Wright. Former Darlington Striker.

"Julian Joachim was my footballing hero. As a kid, I stood on the Kop at Filbert Street, watching Julian terrorise defences. I was a striker, like him, and I idolised him. My dad had a printing business that sponsored Julian, so I got to meet him as a fan which was pretty cool.

A decade later, I followed in Julian's footsteps and made my Leicester City debut in a Premier League match against Leeds United and my own career began.

In 2007, I was on the verge of leaving Championship side Barnsley when I received an offer from Darlington, who were in League Two. I'll be honest, I wasn't sure about dropping down two divisions and I didn't know much about the club, so I did a bit of research. I went onto their website and looked through a list of their players, stopping when I saw one familiar name – Julian Joachim. For them to have a player of that ilk showed me that they were a serious and ambitious club and I signed for Darlington soon after.

They say that you shouldn't meet your heroes, but Jockey did not disappoint. At the start of my career, I had been fortunate enough to work with Paul Dickov, Les Ferdinand and Dion Dublin, so for me to have the opportunity to play with someone like Jockey, who had been there and done it, was great for me and I learned a lot from him. It's not that he was vocal, far from it. It was more that I had so much respect for the guy and his presence inspired me to up my game. I wanted to outscore him. I wanted to be as good as Julian Joachim. My aim was to get to the level where I could compete with him as I knew that would put me in a very good place.

Playing alongside Jockey was a dream come true. To go from watching him on the terraces to lining up alongside him was very surreal. We weren't regular strike partners because he was often used as a winger due to his pace. Even at 33, he was still lightening fast. Our opponents were terrified of him, often doubling up on him because they were so scared. With two defenders keeping a close eye on him, it freed up space and created many opportunities for me.

Even though he was approaching the end of his career, he still had fantastic ability. I lost count of the number of times he amazed me with his touch, the way he moved and how he carried the ball. He'd pull balls out of the air that no one else could have done and still showed big bursts of pace, even at his advanced years. I was in awe of him and I sometimes had to pinch myself that we were sharing a pitch. I think it's nice that I never lost the passion and excitement that I'd had as a fan.

We didn't socialise much off the pitch because I was quite a lot younger than him, so while I would go into the town and head to the gym after training, Julian would settle in a café with a paper before heading off to the bookies. But when we did enjoy a meal together or go on away trips Jockey was great fun to be around. He didn't necessarily make the jokes, but he was always involved and had this infectious belly laugh.

It was an honour to play with Julian and a pleasure to get to know him as a man."

*****

As it turned out, I was still at Boston when the new campaign kicked off on 5th August 2006 away at Grimsby. Although I scored, we lost 3-2 and I realised that it was going to be a difficult season for us. There had been too many changes and the players who had come in in weren't as good as those they had replaced.

We lost to Peterborough in our next game and then, unbeknown to me, Boston verbally agreed a £50,000 fee for me with Darlington – our next opponents.

I had my best ever game in a Boston shirt, scoring a brace, setting up one and winning the penalty for our fourth goal in a stunning 4-1 win. We absolutely battered them. After the game, I had a quick pint in the bar with the lads and went home, fully expecting to spend a relaxing evening with my family. I had just stepped into my house when the phone rang. It was Steve Evans.

"Jockey, we're in trouble financially and we need to sell you. I've got some of the Darlington board members with me now and they want a word. Do you want to speak to them?"

'Here we go again, another move on the cards,' I thought.

I closed the door, got back in my car and returned to York Street to meet with the Darlington directors. They introduced themselves and asked if I fancied joining them. They'd agreed a transfer fee with Boston - £100,000 as my value had doubled following my performance just hours earlier – and we more or less agreed terms there and then. I didn't have an agent at that stage of my career, so I sorted it out myself. They were offering me £4,000 a week, a huge hike, and although I knew that the move would be a big upheaval, I just couldn't turn down that kind of money so late in my career. Boston needed the money from my transfer fee and I didn't have a future there anyway.

On 14th August, two days after playing against Darlington, I travelled up the A1 with Boston's chairman, Jim Rodwell, to sign for Darlington! En route, I got a call from Steve to say that Hartlepool had also made an offer and he asked me to go and speak to them.

"I'll speak to them, gaffer," I said. "But no matter what happens, I'm still going to sign for Darlington because that's what I've agreed to do."

We did a quick detour to Hartlepool where I spoke with their manager, Danny Wilson, who had once tried to sign me for Bristol City. I liked Danny, but I'd already given my word to Darlington, so I politely declined his offer. I am a man of honour.

We then arrived in Darlington, met with their chairman, George Houghton, and the other board members and they gave me the contract on the terms we had verbally agreed and I signed it there and then. Houghton was a bit of a character and I got on well with him. He'd done his homework on me and knew that I liked the horses.

"I like a bet myself, Julian, but I know the jockeys and the trainers, so I get information, good information," he told me. "I'll put some bets on for you and you'll get some winners, I promise. Don't worry, son, you'll be alright with me." And to be fair to him, he did give me a couple of good tips and I won a few quid which was a nice bonus.

Darlington played in League Two, but on paper, were a bigger club than Boston. They played their home games in the 25,000 capacity Darlington Arena, a magnificent stadium, but much too big for us as our attendances averaged between 1,500 - 2,000. Even the big derby match against Hartlepool in March 2007 only attracted 10,000 fans. The board were also working on getting their own training ground and harboured ambitions of winning promotion to League One. Everything felt right.

My new manager, David Hodgson, gave the following quote to the Darlington website:

"Julian has played at the highest level in the English game. He is very fast and he has scored goals wherever he has been."

'Great,' I thought, 'a manager who wants me.'

Wrong!

Hodgson hadn't been invited to the meeting when everything was agreed. Once I'd signed, one of the directors told me that the manager had arrived so I could go and have a chat with him. I left the boardroom and that's when it all came out – Hodgson didn't want to sign me!

In fact, he didn't even know anything about it and wasn't happy. It was the board who had signed me. Jon Sotnik, the Chief Executive, knew all about me from his time at Boston and he had got my name in the directors' heads, telling them what I could do. When I destroyed Darlington with my performance in that 4-1 win, the board were convinced and decided to sign me, but no one had told Hodgson. Apparently Sotnik and the manager were at war and signing me was seen as a way of the board controlling Hodgson and showing him who was in charge.

I fully get the gaffer's reaction. All managers want to bring in their own players and I was the club's record signing which probably made it worse. I wouldn't have signed if I'd known this beforehand. There is no way I would have joined a club if the manager didn't want me there.

Hodgson was open and honest with me from the start. "Great that you're here because I rate you as a player, but I haven't done this. They have done this behind me back. I'm just putting you in the picture because you need to know. We've had a lot of disagreements behind the scenes and things aren't right at this club."

It was far from ideal, but I was now a Darlington player, so I just had to make the best of the situation.

At least I had joined a good side, with a decent squad and some good youngsters.

David Stockdale was a 20-year-old goalkeeper who had joined us from York City. He later became our first-choice keeper, did really well and earnt himself a big move to Premier League Fulham. He even received a call up to the England squad in 2010.

David Wheater was signed on loan from Middlesbrough and added a bit of quality to our defence. He was another young lad who went on to enjoy a good Premier League career.

One of my strike partners was Tommy Wright, a lifelong Leicester City supporter, who told me that I was his hero when he was a kid. The first time we played up front together, he told me that it was a surreal moment. He was a good lad and we linked up with each other well. He's a policeman now which I certainly wouldn't have predicted.

The lads accepted me, so that aspect was good, but I felt that I was caught in the middle of the battle between the board and the manager. The board had stuck two fingers up to the gaffer by signing me and Hodgson got his own back by naming me as a substitute for my first game. I think it was his way of challenging the board and telling them that he was going to do things his way.

We lost 2-1 to Swindon, so I was named in the starting line-up for our next game, a League Cup tie against Championship side, Stoke City. We were massive underdogs, but despite going down to ten-men early doors, we came from behind to win 2-1, the winning goal scored by yours truly. After that, I was pretty much a regular in the side, playing either up front or out on the right.

Our reward for beating Stoke was an away tie against Reading, who were enjoying their first season in the Premier League. Once again, no one gave us a chance and we were determined to prove a point. We put in a fantastic performance and were four minutes away from an unlikely victory. Simon Johnson had given us the lead from the spot before Leroy Lita equalised. I scored to restore our lead, but Lita equalised just a minute later. I got my second of the game not long after the break and we were well on our way to victory when they got a third equaliser through a dodgy referring decision. Peter Mate clearly played the ball with his hand, but the goal stood. We were so unlucky and lost 4-2 on penalties. Reading played Liverpool in the next round and I was gutted because that should have been us going to Anfield.

I thought David Hodgson was sound and after our difficult introduction, we got on well. Hodgson was in his third spell as Darlington manager, originally joining the club in 1995 after a fantastic playing career that saw him win two league titles and one European Cup with the unstoppable Liverpool team of the eighties. When you consider his background, it's not surprising that he had us playing some good, attractive football. We weren't going to win the league that season, but we weren't anywhere near the bottom either. It was a difficult job for Hodgson because his hands were tied and he had little support from the board.

In October 2006, rumours were flying around the club that Hodgson had put his name forward for another job. I'm not sure if that was true or not, but just days later he was sacked.

Dave Penney, who had enjoyed success with Doncaster, was given the manager's job. I was injured when he was appointed, so didn't meet him for a while. If you were injured, you had to report to the stadium each day to do your fitness and rehab work with the physios while the rest of the lads were off training somewhere else. Penney's immediate focus was on the players who were fit, so I didn't meet him until he'd been at the club for a few weeks which was a bit strange. However, as soon as I was fit, he put me back in the team and I did well. We finished 11th in the league, missing out on the play offs by only six points. I scored 10 goals which was a decent return considering that I had played a lot of games on the right.

At the other end of the table, I was saddened to see my old club, Boston, relegated to the National League. The club seem to have more stability now, and a new stadium, and I hope that they return to the football league soon.

When I returned to Darlington for pre-season ahead of the 2007/08 campaign, I was told that I wasn't in Penney's plans anymore and wouldn't be featuring much. The gaffer never explained why he wanted me out or what had changed from the previous season. I still got on well with the chairman, so I went to see him, and he told me that I could leave, but they wanted a fee for me. I'd been their record signing 12 months previously and they had to try and recoup as much of that back as they could. The problem was that no one would meet their valuation. Lincoln City made an enquiry, and I would have been interested, but they couldn't afford the transfer fee, so the move broke down. I still had a year left on my contract, with an option for Darlington to extend it, so I just got my head down and got on with it. It wasn't the first time that I'd been out of favour at a football club. I had always been able to turn things around before and I didn't see why I wouldn't be able to change Penney's mind.

In July, I suffered an injury during training and was ruled out of our glamourous friendly against Middlesbrough, who were managed by my old teammate, Gareth Southgate. The game took place on a Tuesday night and there was a club rule that we weren't allowed to drink 48-hours before a game.

I was living in a rented apartment on my own, as Kate and the kids had remained in Boston. It was hard not seeing them all the time, so I tried to go out when I could to relieve the boredom. So on the Sunday evening before the match, I met a mate at a local working men's club for a couple of frames of snooker. I had a lager shandy, just one though, because I was driving, and I never drink and drive. There was another player in the snooker club, Alan White, who was there with his mates, so I had a few games with him and then I drove back to my apartment.

The following morning, I was called into the manager's office.

"Where were you yesterday?" Penney asked me in an aggressive manner.

"I went out for a couple of games of snooker," I replied.

"Yes, I know you did. You were drinking too, weren't you? Don't deny it, we've got you on camera," he accused.

"Gaffer, I had one shandy."

"One? Don't lie to me. You were hammered," he said. I was shocked. You can count the number of times I've been 'hammered' on your fingers.

"That's nonsense. I'm not a drinker. You ask anyone who knows me, and they will tell you. Gambler, yes, but not a drinker.

Show me the video or tell me who said that I was drunk because that's bullshit," I challenged him.

"We've got a game on Tuesday, you shouldn't have been drinking," he replied, clearly not listening to what I was saying. "You're getting a fine and a written warning."

Steam was coming out of my ears by this point. In any other job, an employer would need to hold an investigation and have solid proof before disciplining someone. Football is completely different, especially if the gaffer decides that your face doesn't fit. I hadn't broken any rules and it was wrong to punish me when I'd done nothing wrong.

Over the next week, he was on my case a lot and told me that he hadn't decided what fine I was getting. Eventually, he called me in to his office and said, "The club wanted to fine you two weeks' wages, but I fought your corner and got it down to a week which I think is enough." It pissed me off even more that he was making out that he had done me a favour! It was bullshit and a way of trying to push me out, but I paid my fine and took it on the chin. 'What happens now?' I asked myself.

I was still being paid, so I kept working hard in training and when called upon for the reserves and sure enough, after one or two injuries I was brought back into the fold. By that stage we had set our sights on promotion and the gaffer needed my experience. I played well and stayed in the side for the rest of the season. We finished sixth in the league and drew Rochdale in the play offs. I played in both legs, but we lost 5-4 on penalties.

At the end of the season, my contract was up. By that stage I'd had enough of living miles away from Kate and the kids and I'd really missed them. I met the gaffer and told him that if it was up to me, I wouldn't extend the contract. He told me he'd speak to the chairman and they both agreed to release me. I didn't have any worries about finding a new club; I was only 33 and had just scored 9 goals, a decent return, for the sixth best team in the division whilst playing in a demanding position.

I didn't have an agent anymore and it was the first time in my career that I had been without a club. I was still fit and in good shape, but I was beginning to feel my age a bit, noticing that it was taking longer to recover between games. I had no thoughts of retiring, but I did want to ease down a bit and spent the summer waiting for the phone to ring.

There were rumours of interest from league clubs, but I surprised a few people by dropping down two divisions and signing for Kings Lynn who were in the Conference North. After two seasons away from my family, I just wanted to be closer to home. I knew that I was coming towards the end of my playing days and I wanted to take things a bit easier. I'd achieved a lot in my career and didn't feel that I had anything left to prove. If I signed for a pro club, I'd have one or two more years, but dropping down a level might mean that I had three or four because it would be less demanding on my body. At Kings Lynn I'd be expected to train twice a week, play the games and I'd have the rest of the time for myself. It was a local club too, so it was the perfect opportunity for me and it felt like the right thing to do.

I signed for Kings Lynn on 2nd July 2008. The following morning, I awoke with the realisation that I was no longer a professional footballer.

I hadn't really considered what I wanted to do with myself when my football career ended. There was no way I was going to be a pundit and although I ran some coaching sessions for the kids at the school where my daughter taught, coaching wasn't something that interested me. I've always been a laid back character and never one to plan ahead. It's hard to plan too much in football anyway because things can change very quickly. I saw so many players who were regular starters become transfer listed in the blink of an eye. Football is a subjective game that is full of opinions and the manager's opinion is the one that counts. If the manager doesn't rate you, it's very hard to get back into the team. My attitude throughout my career was to work hard, focus on one season at a time and not worry too much about the future.

I found it hard to adapt to not being a full time footballer. Motivation was never an issue. I still had the buzz to play – as I still do today – and I prepared for every game in the same way. It didn't matter if I was playing against Manchester United or Stalybridge Celtic, I still wanted to win.

The biggest challenge for me was fitness. Although I wanted to ease off a bit, I was used to training every day and I found it hard to get to grips with just two sessions a week. I didn't feel as razor sharp or as lively as I had previously and my form suffered. I had just come out of the pro scene, was a bit of a name at that level and I was really disappointed with myself.

The last thing I wanted was to be a failure. I always enjoyed the battle, but Kings Lynn were a small club and I was earning decent money for that level, so I went to see the manager, Keith Webb, and gave him the opportunity to rip up my contract and bring someone else in.

Keith was fantastic, explaining that the club were OK financially and told me to keep working hard and I would come good. It was exactly what I needed to hear and gave me some much needed confidence. I did get better, scored a few goals and my performances improved.

Unfortunately, towards the end of that season, the club were in a mess off the pitch and none of us were being paid. I'd been at Leeds and Coventry when they were experiencing financial difficulties, but it is much harder for clubs lower down the leagues as they have very little money coming in. In the end, we received 50% of the amount that we were owed and I left at the end of the 2008/09 season, having played 38 games and scoring eight times. Sadly, Kings Lynn were wound up at the High Court a few months later which was a real shame for the fans, players and staff.

CHAPTER 18
Only foals and horses

When you're a Premier League footballer, everyone wants a piece of you; agents are trying to see how they can make money from you, sponsors are lining up to give you their products and the media are asking for interviews or a soundbite that they can use. As soon as I retired, they all disappeared. I was a down to earth lad who didn't get carried away with the hype and I was never one for courting fame, so it didn't affect me when I left the public eye. The biggest adjustment that I had to make was financially.

On my way up, my wages jumped from £35 to several thousand pounds a week in just a few seasons – it was great. However, I knew that I wouldn't be at the top forever and that the decline in wages would be just as steep as the rise, so while I was earning good money, I was determined to enjoy it. The kids attended private schools as Kate and I wanted them to receive the best education. I bought some nice cars, designer clothes and we had some fantastic holidays as a family. I had nothing when I was growing up and it was tough, so while I had the opportunity, I wanted to treat myself and my family. With hindsight, I probably should have tucked some money away for a rainy day, but I don't regret any of the things that I bought. The biggest problem that I had was that I developed a bad habit – gambling.

I can remember playing cards for pennies when I was just seven years old. I had a large extended family and we got together regularly. Before long, the cards came out and money would appear on the table, so gambling was in me from a young age. I didn't have a great deal of money then, so it was OK and just a bit of fun. But later on, when I was earning good money, I fell into the trap. It started off with 50p or £1 on a horse, then it became a fiver, and as my wages increased so did my bets. It wasn't that I was laying down huge sums of money on one horse, the issue was that I was consistently gambling, having a flutter most days on quite a few races. I'd usually start the first few races at £60, then it would be £100 quid and maybe £200 if I really fancied something. If I was having a good streak and picking winners, I might go to £800. The biggest bet that I placed was £1,500 on a well fancied horse. It sounds a lot – and it is – but I saw others backing it for much larger sums. The horse came in, too!

When I was a YTS player, we trained in the morning and did our chores in the afternoon. It was hard work and long hours, so by the time I returned to my digs I was usually too exhausted to do anything else. It was totally different when I became a pro as we'd train in the morning, have lunch and then I had the rest of the day to myself. Kate would be at work, the kids were at school so I had all this time on my hands and I'd wonder what to do. A lot of players got into golf, for others it was gambling and once you're involved, it's very difficult to get out of.

Gambling is a big thing in football. I don't know what it's like now, but in my day every team had a card school. At Leicester, we played three card brag on the coach to away games. The stakes were only a pound or two, nothing major, it was just to kill some time really. But when I moved to Aston Villa, it was a completely different story.

The card school at Villa was located at the back of the coach, so on my first journey with the lads I was curious to see what was happening. I'll always remember the first time I walked down the aisle towards the rear of the coach and Brian Little, who knew that I liked a flutter, told me to be careful and then instructed Mark Draper to look after me. The gaffer knew that I wasn't on much money compared to the other lads and he didn't want me to get too carried away.

The lads played a form of poker and I watched them for about 15 minutes to see how it worked and I was blown away. I couldn't believe the money that was flying around. A week's wage for me could be won or lost in one hand. It was big money, but I've always enjoyed the buzz of a bet so of course I got involved. I did alright, too. I had my losing days, of course, but I knew that a winning run was always around the corner and more often than not, I managed to win a few quid. It was great fun.

We played whenever and wherever we could and away games were ideal. We mainly travelled on a coach, or plane for European ties, so there were two to three hours in which to play cards. When we arrived at the hotel, we'd grab a bite to eat and then play a few more hands in the evening. A couple more rounds on the coach on the way to the stadium and then a few more hours on the journey home. You could win or lose £10,000 on one trip – serious cash!

You didn't take all your stake money on the coach, you had to bring an amount of cash to buy in, say £300, and then when that ran out – which it did quickly – you'd take money out of the pot (like an IOU) and someone would keep a record, so that at the end of the game you'd know how much you owed or who owed you and you'd usually settle up the following day, with a deal done for cash. So, if you were owed £5,000, you'd accept £4,500 for cash. There were never any rifts and no one ever fell out over cards. Everyone always paid what they owed.

There was no pressure to be part of the card school and you could pull out at any time if you wanted to. Most of the lads had a budget in mind and stuck to it. It never ever affected our performances. Once we crossed that white line, everyone was totally focussed on the match. We had a great team at Villa, a good set of lads and I actually believe that the card games helped to relieve some of the stresses that come from playing Premier League football.

I enjoyed the social aspect of the card school, but my biggest thrill came from betting on the horses. At most of the clubs I played for, we would occasionally have team outings at a racecourse, and they were usually good fun, but I also enjoyed going to the races on my own. There are some colourful characters involved in horseracing and I met some wonderful people, bookies and punters alike.

One such character was Raymond Winterton, known as 'Racing Raymond', a lovely guy who sadly passed away in 2016. He was an on-course bookmaker who went all over the country to most of the major meetings and he often had some good bits of information that he'd share with me over the phone. I spoke with him most days and he became a bit of a father figure and a good family friend. We had some fantastic days out together. He really used to look out for me and I remember him warning me of the dangers of gambling, but I didn't listen and over the years I got a bit too involved. When I was at Leeds, he wrote me a letter advising me to look after my money, not to blow it and he told me to calm down with my betting. Bookies often have a bad reputation, but Racing Raymond was one of the good guys.

I loved everything about the racecourse; the sounds of the horses galloping past, the smell of the turf and the thrill of backing a winner. The buzz that I got from gambling was the closest thing that I have found to the feeling I got when scoring a goal.

When I was at Villa and earning good money, I paid £15,000 for a third share in a racehorse named Native Affair, trained by the legendary Len Lungo. The first time that he ran he finished third and won his second race by a few furlongs. In his third race, Native Affair won by an even greater distance and we were all excited, thinking that we had a decent horse on our hands.

We sent him to Aintree during the Grand National week and he ran a good race, finishing 10th, decent considering he was competing against the best horses from all around the country. We then moved him on to hurdles, but on his first race the horse in front fell which meant that our jockey had to swerve and, sadly, Native Affair picked up an injury and was never the same again. We tried everything we could, but he kept bleeding from his nose any time he came under pressure, so we retired him. I enjoyed my short spell as a racehorse owner, had a bit of fun and made a couple of quid, too.

Over the years, I lost a fair bit through gambling. I wish that I'd taken up golf as a hobby as it would have kept me out of the bookies and saved me a load of trouble. I did try it during my playing days and joined in the various charity golf events that I was invited to, but I couldn't even hit the ball! I'd take big swings to try and hit it as hard as I could, but I was shocking and the lads took the piss! I've recently started playing golf regularly and although it's a hard game full of frustration, it's a good way to pass the time with some mates and have a chat.

I also lost money through some badly advised investments. In the late nineties, the government introduced film partnership schemes with the aim of generating investment in the UK film industry. I, like many other footballers at the time, was advised to invest some money in the schemes, but it turned into an absolute nightmare and I had the tax man on my case big time. It got so bad that by the time I joined Darlington, I was being chased for a six-figure tax bill which was a phenomenal amount. Darlington put me in touch with Gerald Krasner, the chairman of Leeds United at the time, who helped me to declare myself bankrupt. It was my only option.

It was unfortunate, but players are so immersed in football and there are so many scams out there that we need advisors to help us invest our money in the right places. These types of schemes are really complicated and I just had to trust my advisors and hope that they gave me the correct advice. They didn't and I paid the price.

Another investment that I made was in some commercial property, land and foreign apartments which was all arranged through the PFA. It was another gamble, I suppose, although it should have been safer than the horses, but that didn't work out either. I've had no returns and I have a substantial amount of money wrapped up that I can't get back. I'm currently battling away trying to get it resolved. I doubt I'll get my initial investment back, but it would be nice to get something. Whether I do or not is another matter.

It's frustrating, but it's just one of those things and I'm certainly not bad mouthing the PFA. I think they are great for players and you know that they are only a phone call away if you need them. I pumped money into my PFA pension from the age of the 17 and that is one of the few investments that I made that worked out well!

It's hard to recover from bankruptcy and when I was 40, I decided to sell all my memorabilia. I was reading the *Leicester Mercury* one day when I came across an advert for football memorabilia and I thought, 'I've got a few bits and bobs,' so I made a phone call and sold the lot. I'd lost my FA Cup medal in the process of moving house and while my England caps and a couple of shirts were framed and on display at home, the rest of my stuff was tucked away in the loft. I'd already given away a hell of a lot of shirts, and I've never really been sentimental about things, but it was still sad to see it go. I've still got the memories though and no one can take those away from me.

Kate and I have been together for many years now and she has been by my side through the good times and the bad. That's what relationships are all about. She's had to adjust and we've got through everything together. We are a good, strong family unit.

At times, it has been tough, but I know that many others have had it much harder than me. People may look at me and say that I shouldn't be in this position. That I should have looked after my money, made the right investments and not gambled a lot away. Maybe they are right, but that was my choice and I have no regrets. I am happy with my life, have five kids who have turned into wonderful people and I've been blessed with two beautiful grandchildren. That is what is important to me.

Writing this book has given me the opportunity to look back on my career and life. When I think back to when I left Boston as a 16 year old to try and achieve my dream of becoming a professional footballer, I had no idea how things were going to pan out. The only target that I ever set myself was to be a footballer and I achieved that. Everything else was a massive bonus. In the early stages of my career everything went so well for me. Everything! I scored over 100 times as a professional and had an average of a goal every four games. I'm incredibly proud of the career that I've had and I realise how fortunate I have been. After all, I could have spent the last 30 years in a farmer's field picking Brussels sprouts and catching chickens for a living!

CHAPTER 19
The best of the best

Taking this stroll down Memory Lane has reminded me of the many great players I am blessed to have played with and against. Here are my all-time best eleven teammates and opponents.

My All-Time Teammate Eleven

Formation: 4-4-2

Goalkeeper: Mark Bosnich
On his day, Bossy was unbeatable and he won us so many points by pulling off incredible saves. A loud character who gave me the nickname 'Jockey Fart Pants.'

Right back: Pontus Kamark
Pontus signed for Leicester at the start of my final season at Filbert Street, so I didn't get to play with him as much as I would have liked, but he oozed quality. Pontus was so professional in his approach to the game, almost ahead of his time.

Centre back: Gareth Southgate
Gareth was a ball-playing defender who would have been even better if he was playing today. A real leader on and off the pitch and I'm not surprised that he has done so well as England manager.

Centre back: Sol Campbell
Sol was the complete defender and an absolute colossus at the back. He got into the Spurs first team at an early age and looked like he'd been playing there all his life.

Left back: Alan Wright
Like many of my Villa teammates, Wrighty was a very underrated player. He was a good defender who got forward to join the attack at every opportunity. He set up quite a few goals for me, including the impossible angle goal I scored against Coventry.

Right midfield: Paul Merson
Merse was just quality. He was skilful, strong and had the ability to create a chance from nothing. A good laugh off the pitch too. He was coming to the end of his career when he joined Villa and it's frightening to think how good he must have been during his peak.

Centre midfield: Paul Scholes
Scholesy was one of the most technically gifted players that I have ever seen. Even at 17, he could do things that no one else could. His touch, vision and passing ability were outstanding and his finishing was up there with the very best.

Centre midfield: Jamie Redknapp
Jamie was another who just had bags of natural ability. He was hard working and possessed tremendous passing ability. He achieved a lot in the game, but I think he would have been even better had his career not been hampered by injury.

Left midfield: David Ginola
The third foreign player in the team, David had a magical touch and was gifted with the ability to breeze past defenders as if they weren't even there. He is another player who scored some spectacular goals.

Striker: Dion Dublin
My favourite striker partner, Dion helped me massively when he joined Villa from Coventry and my game improved no end. He was fantastic in the air and I scored a lot of goals from his flick ons. It is no coincidence that I enjoyed my best goalscoring season playing up front with Dion.

Striker: Dwight Yorke

Yorkey used to amaze me every day in training with his skills and ability. He was a confident lad, but he always backed it up on the pitch. Defenders were scared to death of him and used to double up which created space for me to exploit.

Manager: Brian Little

The man who gave me my first team debut always looked out for me. He helped me with my first contract, came with me to buy my first car and brought me back to the Premier League when he signed me for Villa. Brian was a fantastic manager who achieved a lot at Leicester and Villa.

*****

My All-Time Opponents Eleven

Formation 3-4-3

Goalkeeper: Peter Schmeichel

The best goalkeeper to have played in the Premier League, Schmeichel commanded his defenders well, was brave and had razor sharp reflexes. I managed to score past him a couple of times which is no mean feat and I even played against his son, Kasper, when I was at Darlington.

Centre back: Marcel Desailly

A World Cup winner, European Championship winner, Champions League winner – Marcel won the lot. Sadly, he is also an FA Cup winner having beaten us in the 2000 final. A tough opponent who was fast, strong and read the game so well.

Centre back: Rio Ferdinand

I first played against Rio when he was a youngster breaking into West Ham's team and he was incredible even then. He had everything in his locker; could pass, tackle, was quick, brave and a true leader.

Centre back: Stuart Pearce

Although he spent the majority of his career as a left back, I just couldn't leave him out of this team. He was one of the toughest opponents that I ever came up against. He knew all the tricks and stopped at nothing to prevent you going past him.

Right midfield: David Beckham

I played alongside Becks many times at the start of his career and, although he was obviously good, I had no idea that he would go on to become the player that he did. His crossing is by far the best the Premier League has ever seen and he also scored some incredible goals.

Centre midfield: Steven Gerrard

He was one of the best midfielders in the world at his peak. He had so much energy, was a great leader, could tackle, pass, score goals – the list goes on. A top, top player.

Centre midfield: Paul Scholes

The only player to make it into both of my teams which tells you how highly I rate him.

Left midfield: Ryan Giggs

Giggs burst onto the scene around the same time as I did. He was a tremendously skilful winger who twisted many a defender inside out. He managed to maintain his incredibly high standards and played top-flight football well into his forties. Amazing.

Striker: Thierry Henry

One of the greatest players ever to play in the Premier League. He was so fast, skilful and had a knack for scoring spectacular goals. He's one of the players who made me glad that I wasn't a defender!

Striker: Alan Shearer

Shearer was an old-fashioned centre forward. Strong, brave, good in the air and had natural finishing ability. Defenders always knew that they'd been in a game when they came up against Shearer.

Striker: Dennis Bergkamp

Bergkamp was a magician with the ball. He made everything look so easy, it was almost like he was playing the game in slow motion. He was one of those players that you just sit back and admire.

Manager: Sir Alex Ferguson

The most successful British manager of all time. Under his leadership, Manchester United were entertaining but also very hard to beat. Funnily enough, I always used to do well against United, even though the teams I was playing for didn't beat them too often.

*****

So, there you go. Two very strong teams. I'm not sure which side would win, but it's certainly a game that I'd enjoy watching.

Acknowledgements

So, that's it. My life story in a book.

When I think back to when I was 16 years old, leaving home for the first time to try and achieve my dream of becoming a professional footballer, I couldn't begin to imagine that I would go on to score at Wembley, play in an FA Cup final, represent England at various youth levels, winning a tournament, score over 100 goals across all four divisions and play in front of thousands of fans chanting my name. It is only now when I reflect on my life that I realise just how much I accomplished during my career.

I want to take this opportunity to thank some very special people;

Firstly, my mum and nan for believing in me and for the sacrifices that they made in order for me to achieve my dream.

Brian Little for giving me my big break at Leicester City and for his advice and guidance over the years.

My former teammates, coaches and managers – way too many to mention here, but particular thanks to Ian Blyth, Chris Bart-Williams, Gary Mills, Mark Tinkler, Bobby Davison, Iwan Roberts, Stef Oakes, Dion Dublin, Brian Little, Ian Taylor, John Eustace, Dean Gordon, Brian Deane, Lawrie Dudfield and Tommy Wright for providing their memories and stories for this book and to Mark Draper for writing the foreword.

The supporters of all the teams I have ever played for. I always gave 100% in every match and I hope that I have left you with some wonderful memories.

Clive Turner for his friendship over the years and for his generous support through sponsoring this book.

Mathew Mann for listening to my stories and turning them into this book that you are reading now.

All my friends and family – again, too many to mention, but you know who you are.

Kate, my children: Jadine, Roche, Jazzie, Layla, Ziggy, and my two grandchildren: Grace and Giann'a.

And finally, a huge thank you for everyone who has bought this book. I hope that you have enjoyed reading my story.

Julian Joachim

Julian has collaborated with Mathew Mann to write his autobiography. Mathew has written several books, including What If? An Alternative History of Leicester City and "Minding My Own Football Business" by Barrie Pierpoint.

Mathew would like to thank:

Julian for taking me into his confidence and for giving me the opportunity to ghostwrite his book.

My wife, Holly, and my children, Dylan and Eve. You are my inspiration.

Career statistics

	Appearances	Goals
Leicester City 1992 - 1996	92 + 27 sub	31
Aston Villa 1996 - 2001	114 + 59 sub	45
Coventry City 2001 - 2004	46 + 14 sub	14
Leeds United 2004 - 2005	13 + 18 sub	2
Walsall 2005	8	6
Boston United 2005 - 2006	42 + 2 sub	19
Darlington 2006 - 2008	76 + 11 sub	16
England (Under-19) 1993	4 + 2 sub	2
England (Under-18) 1993	6	3
England (Under-21) 1994 - 1995	8 + 1 sub	1
Total	**416 + 135 sub**	**139**

Honours

FIFA Youth World Cup	Third Place	1993
Divison One Play Off	Runners Up	1993
UEFA Under 18 European Championships	Winners	1993
Division One Play Off	Winners	1994
League Cup	Winners	1996
FA Cup	Runners Up	2000

Leicester City **Young Player of the Year**	1993
Under 18 European Championships **Goal of the Tournament**	1993
Under 18 European Championships **Player of the Tournament**	1993
Aston Villa **Player of the Year**	1999
Coventry City London Supporter's Club **Player of the Year**	2004

MORGAN LAWRENCE
PUBLISHING SERVICES

The following books are also available to purchase from
morganlawrence.co.uk and all major book retailers

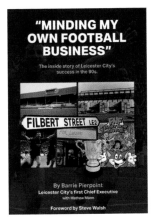

Minding My Own Football Business
By Barrie Pierpoint

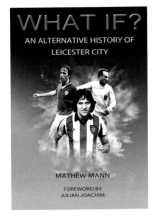

What If?
By Mathew Mann

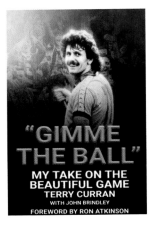

Gimme The Ball
By Terry Curran

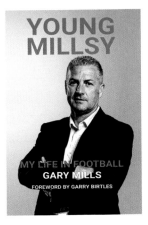

Young Millsy
By Gary Mills

Email: hello@morganlawrence.co.uk
Telephone: 07514 116 493

Roofing & Builders

Presented by
Clive Turner

T: 0116 2419137   **M:** 07860 419137
E: roofingandbuilders@hotmail.com
Safe Construction (LEICESTER) LTD
10 Pulford Drive, Scraptoft, Leicester LE7 9UD

What we do

Re-Roofs / New Roofs / Flat Roofs / Factory Cladding
Roofs / Flat Roof to Pitch Roof Conversion /
Roof Repairs / Slating & Tiling / Extensions /
Ventilation Systems / Conservatories / Porches /
Garden Walls / Chimneys Reduced or Rebuilt or
Repointed / Block Paving / Windows /
Fitted Kitchens / New UPVC Gutters & Facias Etc.